Sociology of Media

Impact of Doordarshan on Tribals

Sociology of Media

Impact of Doordarshan on Tribals

Sushil Kumar Sinha
Research Officer
Ministry of Social Justice & Empowerment
Government of India, New Delhi

Raj Publications
Delhi - 110009 (INDIA)

Sociology of Media: Impact of Doordarshan on Tribals

First Published in 2004

ISBN 81-86208-33-X

Published by : ***Poonam Goel***
Raj Publications
R-115/2, Model Town - III,
Delhi - 110009
Tel. : 011- 27143321
Email : rajpub@now-india.net.in

Laser Typesetting : Aarati Computers,
Delhi-110 009

Printed at : Chawla Offset Printers,
Delhi-110 052

PRINTED IN INDIA

Dedicated

to

my mother

Smt. K.P. Devi

Preface

Social scientists have termed this decade as the decade of communication, and convergance of technology in this field is going to play an important role in bringing changes in the society. One of the important pillars of communication is mass media, i.e.; Doordarshan which is seen as a purveyor of social change. Doordarshan with its modest beginning on 15th September' 1959 went a long way to come to this age. In this period it has seen many ups and downs. From government controlled institution it became an autonomous institution on 23rd November' 1997 under **Prasar Bharti**, so that it can fulfill its obligations towards mass of this country in more better way with its 1325 HPTs spread all over the country. Despite competitive pressure from the market driven private channels and their clamour for high rating and quick pickings it steadfastly continued to be the quintessential public service broadcaster. Communication historians have long argued that changes are arrival through development in new technologies in mass media. Arrival of mass media especially TV has transformed the cultural landscape. Beliefs attitudes, prejudices and established pattern of behaviour all are influenced by it. For the last fourteen years, I have been associated with the **Research Wing** of this esteemed organization and has gone through many research projects involving assessment of different programmes and also the needs and requirements of its audiences, but I could not find any indepth study on subject of this importance, from the Doordarshan community, which inspired me to do an indepth study so that it could be beneficial for all those who are interested in the study in the field of electronic media. The topic of this study includes different aspects related to the impact of Doordarshan on tribals who are in the process of continuity and change.

To say that the electronic media are undergoing rapid change has been accepted in different corner. The combination of digital broadcasting technology, audio/video streaming on the internet and deregulation is totally reshaping the landscape for both the new and existing electronic media. As we enter the first decade of the 21st century, consumer will enjoy a vast new array of entertainment and information sources never before available; but Doordarshan with its vast terristerial reach will maintain its number one position in the country and it is constantly improving its services according to individual tastes and needs.

26 January, 2004 — *Sushil Kumar Sinha*

Acknowledgement

My effort has been to make this book a little different as lots of books on Electronic Media are already available in the market narrating various stages of growth of Doordarshan but this is an indepth unique study of Doordarshan impact on the tribals because from time immemorial tribals have been treated step motherly and looked down upon by the developed sections of our society.

In many areas they were living in isolation but now they have joined the mainstream of society. Many untouched aspects of tribals life influenced by Doordarshan programme has been dealt in this book. I have tried to be as objective as possible, but human nature being what it is, some bias is inevitable in its presentation. I hope that this book will be helpful and put to more effective use by all those who are concerned with media study in one way or the other.

I owe my sincere gratitude to Dr. Kali Nath Jha, Lecturer, Department of Sociology, Mandar College (Ranchi University, Ranchi) who inspired me to do this work and without his full co-operation, I could not have done a work of such nature and magnitude.

I am thankful to the Head of Sociology, Deptt; Ranchi University; Dr. Sharad Kumar, who extended his full co-operation whenever I sought it. He also gave me free hand to use the deptt. library in connection with my work. Last but not the least, I am also grateful to my parents and especially my wife who despite nurturing two youngers and day-do-day problems encouraged and inspired me at every step in completing this work. I am also thankful to my seniors and colleagues and the viewers of my study, without whose help I could not have done this work smoothly and tension free.

— *Sushil Kumar Sinha*

Contents

1

Introduction

Doordarshan, the national television service of India devoted to public service broadcasting is one of the largest terrestrial networks in the world. Doordarshan uses a large number of transponders on the INSAT and other satellites to network its terrestrial transmitters and also to provide additional satellite channels. Doordarshan programmes are watched in India by 362 million viewers in their homes. The first telecast on Doordarshan originated from a makeshift studio at Akashvani Bhawan, New Delhi on 15th September 1959.

Doordarshan has tried to establish a three tier primary programme service - national, regional and local. In the national programmes the focus is an events and issues of interest to the whole nation. The regional programmes originating from the state capitals and relayed by all transmitters in the respective states have programmes of interest at the state level, in the language and idiom of that particular region. The local programmes are area specific and cover local issues featuring local people. At each tier there is a mix of information, education and entertainment programmes. On the national network, news bulletins are telecast in Hindi and English on the hour. It has a number of programmes on current affairs where topical issues are discussed in-depth, bringing out various viewpoints. Information programmes also include telecasts on agriculture, rural development, health, family welfare, consumer's rights, environment etc. There are programmes specially targeted to women, children and youth. In addition to these programmes, Doordarshan brings to its viewers all the major national and international sports and games through live telecasts. There are programmes on sports, including interviews with eminent sports persons, sports education etc.

All India Radio and Doordarshan functioned as departments under the Ministry of Information and Broadcasting till the Parliament passed an act to give autonomy to the media in 1990 itself, but at that time the act was not notified. In 1997 the government decided to notify this act and Prasar Bharti, the autonomous Broadcasting Council of India, came into existence on 23rd November' 1997.

The tribes of India divided into three categories in terms of their ecological, economic and cultural development have been differently affected by the modern process of change. However, with the accelerating impact of urbanization, industrialization and modernization, agricultural economy is surely but slowly undergoing transformation.

The processes of rearing up and socialization among most of the tribes of India is similar in nature. The birth of a male child is considered to be good. Children are weaned when they attain the age of about two years. Only a few weeks after the birth of a child the mother starts her regular household work. She carries the child always on her back by fastening the child in her Sari or with the help of another big piece of cloth. From early youth, the tribal listen to his myths and lore, and though he receives negligible education of a formal nature he learns as he grows up, first in the family and later in the larger circle of the village and the tribe to acquaint himself with the social values and ethics that govern the tribal life.

The tribal cultures of India have undergone radical changes in the past years after independence. These have a direct bearing on the gradual decay of social solidarity in the tribal village.

The process of urbanization among the tribals are involving changes in several dimension. The primary change is noticed in the occupational sphere which directly induces the change in economic and technological spheres, but it is accompanied by associated changes in the field of social relations, customs, habits and of the values and beliefs. It is interesting to note that the almost all tribal region are known for its mineral resources and natural beauty not only in their respective states but also in the country.

In this context, to accelerate the socio-economic and cultural development of the people including tribals the necessity for setting up the latest and most effective electronic medium like Doordarshan in this area was a long felt need. For examples, the Ranchi Doordarshan was commissioned on priority basis in Ranchi town on 26th September, 1984. It was the second station in the TV map of Bihar (now Jharkhand). The primary coverage area of this centre is 80 km. radius, which roughly covers the entire district of Ranchi and other areas around Ranchi district which includes partly the districts of Singhbhum, Hazaribagh, Giridih, Gumla, Lohardaga and Palamau.

In this context it is important to co-relate between the function, impact and the viewers of Doordarshan. For example Jharkhand established as a new state and after being gaining the statehood the process of industrialization, urbanization, modernization has gained highly momentum. The social relations are changing and the situation is changing very fast and the speed of development is very high in general and in infrastructure in particular. In this situation, Doordarshan plays a vital role to educate the people and produces a lot of entertainment and awareness, programmes.

In this context, the present study--impact of Doordarshan on tribals is highly important from sociological point view.

II

Concept

Sociology of media—The study of formal systems for encoding, storing and transmitting information has three distinct aspect.

(i) Audience Research

Since the 1930s newspaper and magazine publishers have carried out regular programmes to discover who reads their product. Governmental concern with both the extent and nature of the impact of public information and propaganda services during the war years accelerated and broadened interest in the nature of media audiences, and the way in which readers, radio listeners and, later, television viewers were influenced by what they read, heard or watched. This focus on media influence and media audiences is quantitatively the most important among sociologists. Among topics frequently studied are the political influence of the media; whether they cause people to act violently; whether they amplify civil disorder; the extent to which readers/listeners/viewers imitate recorded behaviour (e.g. crimes or modes of suicide). Though a rather simple empiricism pre-dominates, answering such questions requires some theoretical model. Three models have been specially influential.

(A) The simple causal model (sometimes referred to as the 'hypodermic' theory) according to which people react directly to media experience (e.g. the representation of killings on television causes murders to happen or the presence of sexist material in newspapers causes men to act chauvinistically).

(B) Models of mediated causality, the best known of which is the two-step flow theory. Within any community there exist opinion leaders, respected figures in key positions whose views are sought and valued. In order to respond to demand such people will be assiduous consumers of media news and views, and act as channels through which media influences and opinions are transmitted; through them the media exert force on the public at large.

(C) Models which deny any independent influence to the media but instead point to processes of selective perception or opinion sets among audiences. According to this view, media audiences are not plastic or readily malleable. Readers, listeners and viewers already hold relatively firm and systematic views of the world, and they shape their consumption of media information in terms of those views; they give the greatest weight to media information which reinforces or serves to confirm positions already held and little or no weight to information which contradicts them.

Research on audiences has been in theoretical content weak but it has been an important area for developing field research technique and has enviably (if narrowly) reliable data series. The lable audience research is normally given to the investigation on behalf of mass media organizations, especially those concerned with newspapers and broadcasting, of the social patterns of viewing and listening. The results are widely used by academic social researchers, despite variations in the quality of data. The practice and the techniqes originated in the USA because of the commercially sponsored nature of radio and, later, television broadcasting services, to provide advertisers with information on the numbers and social characteristics of viewers and listeners. Thus audience research has been principally concerned with who listens to, or watches, or reads, what, rather than how and why. Recent research, particularly by the UK broadcasting authorities, has sought to go beyond this rudimentary question. However, although the research techniques, especially in sampling, are sophisticated, doubts persist about the reliability of all save the most simple information obtained. Nonetheless, the resources devoted to it, the frequency and regularity with which the research is carried out and the size of the samples studied make its use a necessity for most academic researchers in the field.

In the UK the most frequently cited sources are the BBC research department, the Audit Bureau of Circulation, JICTAR and JICRAR. The first is self-explanatory. The second carries out regular routine surveys of newspapers and magazine readership in the UK to provide those who advertise in the press with information concerning the aggregate number of buyers and readers of periodicals and their socio-economic characteristics. The accuracy and availability of this information makes its regular use and citation by social scientists inevitable, but it is important to bear in mind the motives for and circumstances of its collection. It is unfortunate that the intervals and classifications employed (e.g. of social class) differ markedly from those in common academic use. The Joint Industry Committee for Television Audience Research and the Joint Industry Committee for Radio Audience Research carry out roughly comparable functions for the commercial broadcasting system.

(ii) The Study of Media Organization

Research in this field is of more recent origin than that of audiences and has been independent of it. The principle issues have been:

(a) The relationship between personnel directly concerned with generating the content of the media itself and those performing ancillary functions, (e.g. between journalists and newspaper proprietors and managers).

(b) The relation between media organizations, many of which make universalistic claims, and particular interest groups in the environing society.

(c) The mechanisms by means of which media organizations choose which items of information to transmit and which to reject. Borrowing from the language of social anthropology, media organization have been described as gatekeepers, to focus on their function as critical forces in determining the constitution of culture in advanced industrial societies.

(iii) Media Content

Given the complexity of all save the most trivial items communicated in the media, discussion on content has presented acute methodological difficulties for sociological analysis. The cultural substantive question has been whether and to what extent the media represent the ruling ideology of the environing society. The content of the mass media, especially newspapers and television, has attracted the bulk of attention.[1]

Social interaction is dependent upon the passing of messages between actors. Such communication points to an initiative to be taken, a recipient, a mode, content and an effect. This perspective is summarized in a question put in the late 1940s by the American political scientist Lasswell, who says what is which channel to whom with what effect? Inter-personal interaction focuses around communication of two types: verbal and non-verbal. Messages are also increasingly passed under conditions of mass communication through the mass media. In this case the context differs not only from that of inter-personal interaction, but also from that in a crowd, for example a political meeting. Hence the processes involved and the outcomes achieved will be of a very different order from those achieved in small-scale situations. The seeming face to face relationship between listener or viewer and performer in the case of the mass media has been termed a para-social relationship.

III

Tribe, Tribalism and De-tribalization

Tribe—the meaning of this concept shifts uneasily with changing world views. Its earliest and possibly still most colloquial usage refers to a group of people who live in 'primitive or even 'barbaric' conditions under a chief or headman. In the late 19th century, when the belief in evolutionism accompanied colonial conquest and administration, anthropologists defined the social organization of overseas peoples to contrast it with 'modern' societies. The kinship basis of social organization struck Henri Maine (Ancient Law, 1861) and Lewis H. Morgan (Ancient Society, 1877) as a significant contrast with the territorial foundation of the modern state. 'Tribe' came to mean a group connected through descent from a common ancestor, organizes around and ascribed status structure, contrasted with the principle of voluntary contract which appeared salient in modern societies. These contrasts gained the concept of tribe the pejorative overtone of 'primitiveness'.

The needs of colonial administrators to count and classify subject people for taxation and government prompted social anthropologists in the beginning of this century to undertake more detailed study of social groups, especially in Africa. They traced ethnic origins and examined patterns of culture and language, both of which came to be included in the concept of 'tribe'. Of crucial importance in view of later controversies is that it was necessary for administrative purposes to assign individuals to social units larger than the village community which embraced, indeed enclosed, most people's daily lives. Village might be loosely connected on the basis of common recognized descent, even language and customs, but rarely shared a common social purpose in activities such as trade and welfare. They were an ethnic cultural grouping, rather than a social, political or economic organization. Colonial administrators imposed administrative unity upon these cultural and ethnic groupings, creating and naming 'tribes'.

Nevertheless, in contemporary post-colonial Africa tribes do exist, and are relevant in the study or design of national development—despite the rhetoric wisdom of most African political leaders, as well as the deeply held conviction of many African writers. Indeed, social scientists everywhere have started to shun the word 'tribe', preferring the less politically sensitive 'ethnic group'. Yet the very fact that the colonial administration gave no recognition to what were perhaps only loosely connected ethnic and cultural groupings made the tribe an objective reality which has imposed limits to national development in post-colonial Africa.

Tribalism

The subjective awareness of one's membership of a tribe. As in any group dynamics, the sense of belonging and security associated with the 'we' group derives strength and vitality from the contrast and the conflict with the 'they' group, as Sumner argued. Tribalism refers to tribal rivalries in the context of the fragile national alliances of contemporary African states. Paradoxically, inter-tribal conflict and welfare has increased since independence. For all the colonial powers 'creation' of the tribes, their mutual antagonism toward the colonial rulers held the people of diverse tribes together in a common cause which has not yet been replaced by allegiance to a national community.

De-tribalization

With the spread of modern (western) values, of industrialization, and of urbanization with its associated phenomena or geographical and social mobility, tribal people increasingly participate in a wider, more generalized culture and in a plural social community. As participation and mobility reduce the degree of social cohesion of the tribe commitment of the individual, we speak of de-tribalization.

IV

Earlier Literature

There are so many studies and surveys been conducted in this regard. In this connection, the media studies mentioned above have been analyzed by the author.

Yogendra Singh has analyzed the media impact very rightly with reference to globalization. He writes that, 'Besides the major telecommunication means, viz., radio, television and films, the role of telephones, mobile phones, e-mail, fax, internet, etc., is also expanding. The radio, even today, continues to be the most accessible mass-based medium. In 1997, it had 187 stations, 297 transmitters and covered 94.5 percent of population. It broadcasts educational, developmental, informative and entertainment oriented programmes in almost all regional languages of India. In addition, it also broadcasts programmes of national interest including regular news. There are local, regional and national channels, besides an external services division, which cater to various types of entertainment, information and developmental needs of expatriates. Specific programmes for children, women, farmers and on matters related to health, sports, etc. have a priority in radio broadcasts. There is emphasis on promotion of both classical cultural forms of music, dance and drama etc. as well as the folk, regional and local cultural formats. But, the popularity of film-based songs and dance sequences remains on the top. Such programmes are beamed by both radio and television.

Films have played a very important role in India, and even today remain the most popular form of entertainment and recreation. They have also played a crucial part from time to time in promoting educational and reformative values. They have proved to be a major source of linguistic and cultural integration. To regulate their content and form in tune with the normative standards of society the government has established a Central Board of Film Certification. In 1996 alone 683 films were produced in 23 languages including Spanish. The five major languages in which maximum number of films are produced include: Hindi (126), Tamil (138), Telugu (154), Kannada (86) and Malyalam (65). Films have also been produced in languages of smaller communities reflecting local or regional cultures such as Manipuri, Konkani, Urdu, Garhwali, Rajasthani, etc. The Indian television, also known as Doordarshan, draws heavily from film-based programmes. Doordarshan, which made a modest beginning in 1968 with the objective of showing educational programmes for social and economic development of society, has rapidly expanded during the last two decades of the present century. With the availability of satellite facilities it runs three types of transmitters: very high power (77), low power (534) and very low power (153).

Between 1982 and 1995, India launched eight INSAT-series satellites which have contributed to a massive expansion of the Doordarshan coverage to 846.5 million of the total population (Annual report, I & B Ministry, 1996-97). Doordarshan now has eighteen (now 23 Satellite channels) channels: DD-1, which beams national, regional, local and educational programmes, DD-2, which was an entertainment channel, now converted to DD-News channel. DD-3, which is the infotainment channel with programmes on culture and current affairs, Regional Languages Satellite Service (RLSS) which offers programmes to promote regional and local languages, the DD-India, which offers international services to 50 countries, the DD Movie Club (in the past) and DD-CNNI offering

24 hours current affairs programmes. In addition, there is state network which beams Hindi programmes to concerned states. Now, about 60 million homes have TV sets with viewer-ship of 415 million. Doordarshan has maintained more than 80 percent viewer-ship in urban areas and 95 percent in rural areas despite opening of the foreign channels.[2]

Yogendra Singh further writes that India, with its new policy of liberalization and privatization of telecommunication, is now moving fast towards global linkages--economic, cultural and social.[3]

Other studies are also to be noted here. One study conducted by Biswajit Das. It is a report entitled 'Mass Media'.[4]

Another important study conducted by H.I. Schiller entitled 'Current Views of Information and Media Power'.[5]

Despite these studies, time to time Doordarshan has conducted a number of audience research surveys in this regard.

V

Main Objectives

The situation is changing very fast and in this context the impact of Doordarshan on tribals in different perspective is highly important to study in-depth from sociological point of view. Hence, the main objectives of this study are as follows:

(i) To throw light on the relationship between tribal community and Doordarshan and their exposure to this media.

(ii) To analyse the impact of Doordarshan on tribals toward educational social, cultural, economical, as well as political developments.

(iii) To analyse the impact of Doordarshan on tribals towards continuity and change.

VI

Doordarshan : A Microscopic study of Area

The capital city of Jharkhand, Ranchi is located on the Chotanagpur plateau at a height of 2100 feet, and on the map it extends between 23' 25" and 23' 23" latitude and 85' 28" and 85' 23" longitude.

It is bounded on the north by Palamau, Hazaribagh, on the south by Singhbhum and Sundergarh (Orissa), on the east by Singhbhum and Purulia (West Bengal) and on the west by Raigarh and Sarguja (M.P. and Palamau). Geographical factors have greatly contributed to the development of Ranchi into a modern urban centre. The abundance of natural resources around this city has further made it a potential industrial centre. The most important minerals such as coal and iron are found in its vicinity.

Ranchi is also noted for its remarkably bracing climate. Except for about a month or two in summer (April and May) when the heat is somewhat trying, the weather is generally agreeable owing to this climate characteristics. It was a centre of attraction for British officials in the past.

There are three distinct seasons in Ranchi. They are:

The summer season – from March to May

The rainy season – from June to October

The winter season – from November to February.

Ranchi was connected with the national highway (G.T. Road) just after 1834. After this period, roads were constructed from Ranchi to headquarters of the surrounding districts.

Ranchi in course of time become the nerve centre of Chotanagpur, because it was connected by roads from all parts of Chotanagpur. At present, a lot of work in this direction has been done.

The first rail connection from Ranchi to Purulia was started in the year 1908. In the year 1960 by a direct broad gauge railway line upto Muri, Ranchi was connected with Kolkata, Patna and Jamshedpur. Later Ranchi was connected by rail to all important cities of India.

Air services from Ranchi to Patna started as early as in 1951 but after some time it was closed down due to loss of revenue. Recently air services has been again started, connecting Ranchi to Kolkata, Patna, Delhi and Mumbai. It provides a regular services to a number of passengers.

The city in the past was a cluster of isolated tribal villages but now it has emerged as an important industrial and urban region in India. There was a time when the tribals were the chief element of its population but now people from different parts of the state in particular and India in general have formed the core of its present day population.

The rapid increase in population is mainly because recurring waves of migration from village to urban areas and migrants from rural and urban areas of the other districts of Jharkhand and of other states of India. The birth of a number of big industries has also attracted some foreign immigrants and it has been reported that more than a hundred Russians and Czechoslovakian families are temporarily settled at Hatia.

In the past Ranchi was principally tribal inhabited village but in course of time Ranchi has been transformed into a cosmopolitan city. In the past Ranchi city had dominance of tribal population but now with the influx of non-tribal population, its population composition has been greatly changed. The rapidly growing population of Ranchi owing to the increase of various types of industrial, administrative, commercial and educational institutions in and around Ranchi has brought about many demographic changes in the composition and nature of its population.

The spell of industrialization started since 1960 after setting of Heavy Engineering Corporation in Ranchi in the year 1960. Many industries are located in and around Ranchi mention may be made of a few big industries like H.E.C., Usha Martin, Johnson and Nicholson Ltd., Garden Reach (Ship building plant at Dhurwa), Shree Ram Bearing etc. Besides these many medium and small scale industries are situated in and around Ranchi which are mainly located in Tupudana, Tatisilway, Kokar and Mesra industrial areas.

As Ranchi city has been industrialized with the setting of a number of industrial concerns, it has also been urbanized. The wave of industrialization lead to deforestation, displacement, modernization, urbanization etc. In course of time it also witnessed the various problems like other rich cities in India e.g. problem of housing, purity of water, air etc. It all contributed a lot to the problem of pollution.

The influence of urbanization on the behaviour and culture of the people of this city among many other things may be understood in terms of ethnic composition, educational backwardness, poverty etc. The people with different cultural background have prepared themselves differently in accepting the challenges of urbanization and that is why we find that the tribal people though undergoing urbanization have very much resisted and in some cases modified the forces of urbanization owing to their tradition, isolated living educational backwardness, poverty etc. They feel inclined to maintain their exclusiveness and prefer to mix as little as possible with the non-tribals. Increasing growth of this city and an all round urbanization and industrialization around the city, show a definite trend for changing the illiterate agriculturalism to literate industrialism. Ranchi faces the problems of an integrated development of city and its hinterland where the adverse ethnic, religious, and linguistic groups play their mutual and cordial roles sometimes the traditions and norms of these groups especially of the tribal and non-tribal societies appear to be conflicting at least incongruous conformity with one set of norms may lead to conflict with another set. This is the region that the tribals and non-tribals (to a large extent) commonly find it difficult to achieve a satisfied mode of integrated life.

The process of urbanization and industrialization does not affect only the people living within the boundaries of the city, but almost with equal force, it also influences every sphere of the life of the people living in the semi-urban areas such as Namkom, Kanke, Hatia, Buti more and Deepatoli etc. In fact suburbs are as much a part of the city as the area within the city boundary. The semi-urban residents share in the economic and social activities of the city. Many of these have their business or employment in the city, and to a less extent, persons residing in the city are employed in such suburbs like Namkom, Kanke, Hatia etc.

Further, the process of industrialization, urbanization, westernization and modernization has influenced its hinterland and has penetrated in its inner zone, transformation owing to such urban transmission is evident in the neighbouring villages of the city. However, it is also clear that the tradition oriented tribal societies have put much resistance to the forces of urbanization.

References

1. Michacl Mann. (ed.) 'Sociology', 1984.
2. Yogendra Singh, 'Culture Change in India', Rawat, 2000, pp. 57-59.
3. Ibid., p.59.
4. Biswajit Das, 'Mass Media', Report on fifty Years of Communication Growth in India, Mimcographed, 1997.
5. H.I.Schiller, 'Current Views on Information and Media Power' in Christian Academy (ed.), The World Community in Post-Industrial society: Community and Change in Communication in Post-Industrial Society, Scoul: Wooseok Publishing Co., 1188.

2

Doordarshan : A Profile

Doordarshan occupies a unique place in the electronic media landscape of the country. As the national broadcaster, it is mandated to uphold the unity and integrity of the nation and to provide access to all the segments of the population. Doordarshan functions predominantly as a public service broadcaster and is the inheritor of a great tradition. Despite competitive pressures from the market-driven private channels and their clamour for high rating and quick pickings, Doordarshan steadfastly continued to be the quintessential public service broadcaster.

Doordarshan has the national asset of a huge infrastructure and offers a bouquet of channels, with a wide variety of programme offerings. Its reach is stupendous. Its regional language satellite channels are becoming increasingly popular despite tough competition from private satellite channels.[1]

Prasar Bharti

There was a continuous demand that the electronic

media should be made free from the government control and given autonomy in their functioning. The Parliament passed an Act to give autonomy to the media in 1990 itself, but at that time the Act was not notified. It was meant for the establishment of a Broadcasting Corporation of India. The said Act was brought into force w.e.f. 15th September' 1997 and the Prasar Bharti (Broadcasting Corporation of India) was established on 23rd November' 1997.

Doordarshan (DD-1 National Channel)

Doordarshan, a Public Service Broadcaster, is the largest terrestrial network in the world. The service was started on 15th September, 1959 to transmit educational and developmental programmes on an experimental basis with half an-hour programming. A major land-mark was the introduction of colour television in 1982 with Asiad' 82 (9th Asian Games) which ushered in a major revolution in broadcasting in the country. This was followed by a phase of rapid expansion of Doordarshan when, in 1984, DD installed a transmitter in the country more or less every day.

As on 31st May 2002, Doordarshan has 1314 transmitters (1188 for DD 1 + 121 for DD 2 + 5 others) with 56 studio centres and 23 satellite channels (which includes Gyandarshan).

The flagship of Doordarshan-DD 1 (National) operates through a network of 1188 transmitters of varying power, covering 77.5% of the land area and 89.6% population of India.

The primary channel of Doordarshan (Doordarshan-1) has 3 major components of programme contents-information, education and entertainment. The information component consist of News and Current Affairs. The education component is drawn from the contributors from IGNOU, UGC, CIET, SIET and other sponsored programmes like **Turning Point** (Science magazine) and Terra Quiz (a programme on environment). Public Service Broadcasts also form a part of educational programmes which deal with programmes on women's issues and programmes produced by Public Service Broadcasting Trust. The live interactive show "Hum Hazir Hain" presents persons of eminence before the audience as a part of public service broadeast.

Question Hour in Parliament is telecast live on the National Channel. Specific window is earmarked for programme in regional languages between 2.30 pm and 8.00 pm on all week days for public utility programmes and entertainment programmes in the regional languages and dialects. The entertainment programme mainly consists of mid-day daily soaps between 12.00 to 2.00 pm and again between 9.00 pm to 11.00 pm. This includes feature films on Friday and Saturday and regional Award winning films on Sunday.

Doordarshan has made a significant contribution to accelerate socio-economic change, promote national integration and stimulate scientific temper. Being a public service Broadcaster, it strives to carry messages in its programmes on means of population control and family welfare, agricultural information and knowledge, preservation of environment and ecological balance, highlighting the need for social welfare measures for women, children and the less privileged. It also promotes games and sports, and the artistic and cultural heritage of the country.

Doordarshan's Three Tier Service

Doordarshan has a three tier programme service-National, Regional and Local. The emphasis in the national programme is focused on events and issues of interest to the entire nation. The regional programmes are beamed on DD channel from the state capital

Kendras at specific times and also on the 11 Regional Language Satellite Channels (RLSCs) and relayed by all transmitters in their respective states. These RLSCs telecast programme of interest to the state level in the language of that particular region. The Kendras at local stations originate programmes in the local languages and dialects, and the programmes are area specific.

DD-2 Metro

In the beginning, the single Metro service was introduced from the following 4 metro cities:

1. Delhi 9th August 1984
2. Mumbai 1st May 1985
3. Kolkata 19th November 1987
4. Chennai 1st July 1988

The Metro networking took place on 1st April 1993. The DD 2 transmission increased from 3 hrs. to 16 hrs from 15th August 1993. It further increased to 18 hrs w.e.f., 9th August 1999 (Terrestrial 6.30 am to 00.30 hrs).

DD Metro is positioned as an entertainment channel. Efforts are therefore made to procure programmes which provide quality entertainment. At present entertainment programmes covering a wide spectrum of topics are telecast on the channel. The programmes telecast cn DD 2, include detective serial, fiction, talent hunt show, sitcom, tele-shopping, animation, variety, children, talk shows, youth, news based programmes, light music and devotional music programmes.

The revamping of metro channel had been undertaken during the year with a view to countering the ever-increasing challenge posed by other competing satellite channels, which was met with great success, with improvement in reception and TRP rating of DD Metro.

So far as market is concerned, it has started supporting DD-Metro and recently it has been observed that there is a clear cut tilt towards its programmes.

Launch of better quality programmes with innovative formats, imaginative treatment and inclusion of saleable faces from the field of small screen, the TRP graph is also showing an upish trend which ultimately results into fetching better dividents against spot-buy rates.

Every effort is being made to make this trend sustain and grow.

The round the clock DD 2 service from 9th August, 1999 is now available in both digital and analog mode, through 121 transmitters, (HPTs - 44, LPT - 70, and VLPTs-7). The channel now covers 15.2% of the total area and 36.6% population of the country.

The programmes are relayed by major Kendras including Delhi, Mumbai, Kolkata and Chennai from 6.30 am to 12.30 pm on both satellite and terrestrial mode. From 12.30 am to 6.30 pm the telecast is only on satellite.

Now this channel has been renamed as DD-News, which provides news, Current Affairs and some entertainment programmes for the viewers, round the clock.

DD Sports

For the first time in the history of Indian broadcasting, a dedicated Indian sports satellite channel was launched on 18th March 1999 by the Prime Minister. The duration of the transmission in the beginning was 6 hours daily. It was subsequently increased to 12 hours daily from 25th April' 1999 and round-the clock from 1st June' 2000. DD sports channel has now become encrypted from 15th September' 2000.

From 15th August' 2001 the channel has been repositioned as 'Live Indian Sports Channel' for C&S viewers with the objective to bring the best of live Indian and international sporting events. Some of the changes brought about in the Sports channel include showing Indian sports including 'traditional sports', extensive live coverages of sports like cricket, football, hockey and tennis. Another important feature of the new look DD Sports channel is four hours of daily in-house production, at the Central Production Centre (CPC), Siri Fort, of programmes on fitness, quiz contests and attractive packaged programmes based on Bharti's library.

DD Sports is now a pay channel. During the past 2 and ½ years, a number of major national and international events were telecast live, deferred live or recorded. These events include: Sydney Olympics 2000, BCCI Cricket held in India, ICC Knock-Out, Davis Cup, Australian Open, All - England Badminton Championship, Commonwealth Table Tennis Championship, Euro 2000 Soccer, etc.

Doordarshan has entered into an agreement with 16 National Sports Organizations/Federations, including Board of Cricket Control of India, Indian Hockey Federation, All-India Tennis Association on a long-term basis for smooth and planned coverage of the major events organized by them. Apart from national cricket matches, all the international cricket played in India are also being covered by Doordarshan on a 5 - year agreement with BCCI.

The channel earlier available on analog and digital mode on PAS - 4 has now been shifted on PAS - 10 from 6th August, 2001 with footprints in 34 countries of Middle East, CIS and African region.

News and Current Affairs

For the last several decades, Doordarshan news

and current affairs have provided to the viewers, a balanced and objective presentation of day-to-day news and developments covering a wide canvas of issues relating to politics, business, and economics, sports, health, youth, international affairs, science and technology, etc.

As a part of the national network, Doordarshan news and current affairs at present is catering to at least 30 percent time-slot on the channel. It is providing round-the-clock news bulletins with headlines on the hour every hour. In the last one year, with the course of the short-lived independent news channel of Doordarshan, the segment of news on DD-1 has increased appreciably and the duration of the bulletins has also increased. There are now two half an hour long bulletins every morning with live inputs from different regions of the country. The same is available at prime time every evening.

Substantial chunks of news and current affairs, which were out-sourced during the pendency of the news channel, are now by and large in-house. The anchoring and reporting capability has also increased substantially with the induction of 21 Anchors/ Reporters, who form the core group in the headquarters at CPC, Asiad Village and some of whom are being posted to different state capitals to strengthen the coverage span of the network. A major effort is on the anvil to reactivate the regional news units in the state capitals to be more responsive to daily developments and contribute significantly to the overall coverage of news events across the nation. These are now getting reflected as wholesome capsules in the national news bulletins. News segments like newspaper review, business capsule, sports capsule, making the difference, personality of the week and others have been introduced recently. During the course of the major bulletins, news scrolling is available for a quick glance and recap of the major stories of the day. During cricket matches, a running update window of the current score is also available.

The regional news emanating from the state capitals, 18 at present, contribute 71 news bulletins every day. This is an enormous task by any standards. The efforts in all bulletins is moderation in contrast to private channels, who often sensationalise the issues. All these bulletins are produced in-house.

Overall, there is as much as 3 hours and 25 minutes of live news every day on DD 1, 10 minutes of live news in Urdu every day on DD 2 (Now rechristened DD-News) and 3 hours and 35 minutes of live news on DD India every day (This is a combination of the above two). Apart from this, there is invariably a live telecast of breaking stories and special events, such as the annual budget, the exit poll of elections, exim policy and several other live events.

As a sequel to the news presentation, Doordarshan also has a news website, where all the news bulletins are available on line. The website also provides interactive session on select issues. The viewers also have the facility to express their views through the website. It has also an on line stock price ticker and weather information is also available on line. DD news is still in the flux and growing day-by-day the effort is to present news and current affairs with precision and speed but away from sensationalism. The presentation is more slicker and brighter as good as in competitive channels.

DD—Bharti

This new entertainment channel launched by Prasar Bharti on 26th January 2002 is available in the satellite mode, on the PAS-10 satellite, in the band that carried the DD news channel.

The channel focuses on health, children, music, dance and heritage, with special emphasis on the Indian way of life. It carries programmes on yoga, meditation, alternative systems of medicine, aerobics and other aspects of health care in the health segment every day. It holds a daily children and youth segment featuring programmes for the young such as cartoons, talent hunt shows, wildlife films, news magazines by and for children, campus scenes, counselling shows, etc. The channel also offers music, dance, travel and tourism shows, programmes on heritage, and literature.

DD India

To build bridges of communities with Indians living abroad and to show-case the real India; its culture, its values, its tradition, its modernity, its diversity, its unity, its agony and its ecstasy; for the entire world through high quality programmes that will inform, educate and entertain while maintaining the highest traditions of a public service broadcaster.

The DD India channel was launched on 14th March, 1995 with programmes for three hours, five-days-a–week. It is a complete India – centric channel giving an insight into the culture and traditions of India through classical, light and films music; dance; films; news and current affairs programmes; plays and serials, etc. The satellites PAS–9, PAS–10 50° west are used for beaming its programmes. The round-the-clock channel is uplinked from New Delhi.

Gyandarshan—The Educational Channel

Gyandarshan, a major milestone in the field of educational television in India is a joint venture of Ministry of HRD, Information and Broadcasting, the Prasar Bharti and IGNOU. It was launched formally on 26th January 2000. Gyandarshan is envisaged as a public co-operative in which institutions such as the UGC/CEC, NCERT/CIET constitute the major stakeholders.

The Gyandarshan channel, had a modest beginning on 10th January, 2000 with a 2 hours daily test transmission (5 pm to 7 pm). Then on 26th January, 2000 the channel was formally inaugurated. Its duration was increased to 4 hours (5 pm to 9 pm). In mid-February, 2000 the transmission rose to 9 hours a day. By 1st June, 2000 it was extended to 16 hours and by 1st November, 2000 it became a 24 hour channel with non-stop transmission daily offering a rich fare of multi-faceted programming.

The channel has land marked time slot for curriculum–based as well as career based programmes targeting various groups of learners. Special programmes on art, culture, science and technology, etc. having a wider appeal across different age groups are telecast.

The unique feature of the channel is the high degree of interactivity. It is a people's channel which inspires, instills hope and provides the means. Gyandarshan is all set to usher in a learning society. The channel has lent support to the student of secondary and senior secondary school through specially designed programmes by NCERT/CIET, SIET, NOS and others. It also covers topics ranging from science and technology to environment, computer education to career counseling.

The channel seeks to offer alternatives and substitutes to learners of various age groups and categories in the growing demand for quality education in the country.

The 24 hour Gyandarshan channel is now accessible to an estimated 20 million viewers in 40 lakh cable homes spread all over India.

Some New Initiatives

All India Radio and Doordarshan, since their inception have been providing support to national development through a wider variety of programmes reaching the widest possible audience in the country. For several years, a number of campaigns have been undertaken by both media units on their own or on behalf of various Ministries and developments of Government of India.

Consequent upon formation of Prasar Bharti–an autonomous body, Doordarshan and All India Radio are expected to earn a sizable revenue to sustain themselves. At the same time, they have to fulfill the mandate of public service broadcasting. To meet the twin objective in a more focused manner, a cell has been created in Prasar Bharti and named Development Communication Division. This division is offering itself to various Ministeries and Departments as a production house and also a public service broadcaster.

Beginning March' 2001, this division has undertaken a country-wide campaign to highlight various schemes of Rural Development Ministry. This campaign has been conceptualized to be the first ever bi-media campaign in the country creating synergies not only between two media units but also with the field units and extension workers of Rural Development Ministry.

Rural development campaign is targeted at approximately 600 districts and 6 lakh villages in the country for whom the programmes are being broadcast in 29 languages and dialects. Approximately, 2000 personnel from Prasar Bharti are engaged in this campaign from 150 AIR stations and 32 Doordarshan Kendras. Approximately, 1001 programmes and 233 spots were produced for this campaign until 15th November, 2001. In order to create a network for field agancies and to have close interactions with target audience, thus bringing credibility to the media and to the national schemes, a series of orientation workshops were organized at national and regional levels, training approximately 600 participants from Prasar Bharti and concerned Ministries and Departments. Before broadcast, media messages were pre-tested in the field with Audience Research Units of Doordarshan and All India Radio to evaluate the comprehension and effectiveness of the message designed and also to improve upon the production quality of the programmes to be aired. Audience Research Wings of Prasar Bharti also undertook the task of having a baseline survey to know the awareness levels of the target audience about the scheme of Rural Development Ministry. Evaluation study either mid-term or at the end of the campaign provides results that the campaign would have achieved.

Development Communication Division is also doing bi-media campaign on HIV/AIDS in collaboration with BBC and NACO for broadcast in Rajasthan, Uttar Pradesh and Delhi. Yet another campaign on TB, AIDS, Malaria and some other diseases is in the pipeline on behalf of Ministry of Health and Family Welfare.

Now it has taken shape and are telecast from 9 states in the form of "Kalyani". Many baseline & other surveys have been conducted on this telecast by Doordarshan.

Direct to Home Broadcast (DTH)

DTH TV service is a service for direct distribution of television programmes/channels by satellite to the receiving subscriber homes in high frequency Ku band via a small dish and a decoder/set top box. DTH service was banned in India through a notification issued by the Ministry of Communication on 16.7.1997 under the Indian Telegraph Act, 1885 and the Indian Wireless

Telegraphy Act, 1933. The notification prohibited establishment, maintenance, working, possession of or dealing in equipment capable of receiving signals in frequency bands above 4800 MHz (which includes Ku band).

Due to rapid changes in the information technology and sea change in the broadcasting and communication scenario in the last few years, the reasons for which DTH was not allowed in 1997, are no longer relevant. Moreover, DTH is a superior technology, which offers an alternative for distribution and reception of television programmes both to the programme providers as well as to the consumers. Keeping in view its numerous advantages, the matter was re-examined by a group of Ministers. Based on the recommendations of the group, a decision was taken on 2.11.2000 to permit DTH services in India with suitable safeguards so as to take care of the concerns relating to national security, morality and vertical monopoly in distribution.

Convergence Bill

The increasing 'convergence' of technologies have necessisated the urgent need of a statute to regulate the system in India. Accordingly, the cabinet committee passed a bill on 27th August, 2001 and it was introduced in the Lok Sabha on 31st August, 2001. The proposed bill called **'Communication Convergence Bill'** is aimed at promoting and developing the entire communication sector comprising of broadcasting, telecom and multimedia.

Digital Terrestrial Television Broadcasting (DTTB)

At present, there are only two terrestrial TV channels of Doordarshan (DD 1 and DD 2) available in the country, though about 100 satellite channels are being received in different parts of the country. While DD 1 is received in about 76.8% of area of the country covering about 89% of the population, the coverage of DD 2 is available to only about 34.8% population. The terrestrial transmission of Doordarshan is in analog mode. To make more channels available terrestrially in analog mode requires setting up of thousands of transmitters which is just not possible due to limited resources. Therefore, the Prasar Bharti proposes to introduce Digital Terrestrial Television Broadcasting (DTTB) in the country, in a phased manner spanning 10-12 years.

Doordarshan Marketing Division

In view of the highly competitive television scenario, a need was felt for Doordarshan to have an in-house marketing set up, so that - it can be directly in touch with the market. To enable DD to market the channel as a whole rather than in a piecemeal manner. There is single face and identity for DD in the market which was till now being represented through private producers selling an assortment of programmes. To enable DD to market select in-house properties and to package them effectively and reach out and respond to the market requirements as quickly as possible.

International Marketing Division

This division provides material for the sale on programmes/footage to foreign as well as within country as per their requirement, at the approved rate of Doordarshan. It also brings out updated catalogue of in-house programmes from time to time for distribution, to different Embassies as well as different channels. Further, this section co-ordinates the up-linking facilities and provides other technical facilities as per requirement of the foreign/local agancies as per rule through Engineering Wing.

Awards

In the year 2001, Doordarshan instituted Annual award scheme in production, Engineering, Best Doordarshan Kendras and for exemplary work for professional excellence.

There are other two annual awards — Gandhian Philosophy and Public Service Broadcasting. These awards are given on 12th November e.g. Public Service Broadcasting day, the day when Gandhiji visited All India Radio for the first time.

Central Production Centre (New Delhi)

Central Production Centre, Doordarshan was established in 1989 in Asiad Village Complex, Near Siri Fort, New Delhi, as a national production facility, to plan and produce high quality programmes. It was producing more ambitious and complicated types of shows such as - serials, long plays, tele-films, TV documentaries, ballets, light music, devotional music, invited audience programmes, variety shows, TV magazines, games, Kavi Sammelan etc.

CPC has built a rich programme bank covering almost every aspect of our cultural heritage and with some quality entertainment programmes. The programmes of Doordarshan have not only sold to some foreign networks, but also sent to countries with whom they have cultural ties.

Three 24 hours channels are operational from CPC:

1. DD Sports
2. DD India
3. DD Bharti

Doordarshan Kendras in North East

Doordarshan has given priority for the development of TV services in North East. The hilly terrain in this part of the country makes it necessary to have a very large number of transmitters. As on 31st August, 2001 there were 127 transmitters in the North East. There are 11 programme production Centres of Doordarshan in the North-East, Producing Programmes in their languages and also helping in binding people of this region with one another.

Human Resources of Doordarshan

Doordarshan has around 22 thousand employees engaged in programme production, transmission and allied activities. It has establish in-house training facilities and also sends its employees for training in various national and international training institutes like Film and TV Training Institute of Pune and the Asia Pacific Institute of Broadcasting Development of Kualalumpur. In-house training facilities include a Doordarshan Staff Training Institute at Lucknow and the various staff training institutes of All India Radio.

Doordarshan Commercial Service

Doordarshan is a public service broadcaster and hence revenue earning can only be a by-product of its mission and objectives, but it does not undermine the importance of revenue earning. Revenue earning may not be an end itself, but it is a powerful means to its ultimate end. Initially Doordarshan was following the BBC model for funding its activities and owners of television sets were required to pay a license fee of Rs. 50 per annum. Advertisements were not permissible on Doordarshan because of its public service commitments.

However, Doordarshan in 1976 decided to accept commercials in order to supplement its revenue earnings. Hence, from 1976, Doordarshan started to follow a mix revenue model comprising of both the license fee and advertisement revenue. Gradually advertising revenue began to pick up during the decade of 1980, it kept on growing with the organization. As Doordarshan grew by leaps and bounds, so did the advetising revenue. The decade of 1980 brought a kind of revolution for television in India. Colour transmission was introduced w.e.f. 15th August, 1982. Terrestrial coverage expansion was undertaken in a big way. Many new Kendras came into existence.

The decade of 1990 saw an end of Doordarshan's monopoly with the advent of many private and foreign television channels like CNN, BBC, Star, Zee, Sony etc. in spite of highly competitive environment, Doordarshan has been able to successfully safeguard its revenue interests by adopting various pro-active and market-friendly policies. In the year 1996-97 the revenue touched an all-time high figure of Rs. 572.73 crores.

Doordarshan's advertising revenue soared to Rs.637.51 crore during the year 2000-2001. The economic slow-down during 2001-2002 led to the reduction in advertising budget by many big advertisers. The situation got further aggravated due to terrorist attack on World Trade Centre on 11th September, 2001 and on Indian Parliament on 13th December 2001. In spite of these set backs, Doordarshan was able to cross the Rs. 600 crores mark for the second successive year and earned Rs.615.21 crore in the year 2001-2002.

Doordarshan is also working on computerization of its commercial operations for making it more efficient and effective. It is hoped that Doordarshan will be able to maintain its revenue growth without compromising with its public service mandate.[2]

Doordarshan Kendra : Ranchi

Doordarshan Kendra : Ranchi was established in 1984 with the main objective of promoting cultural values of the tribal societies of South Bihar (Now

Jharkhand) and to provide credible and authentic information to the masses. With the creation of Jharkhand State, roles of the two Doordarshan Kendras in Ranchi and Daltonganj respectively along with net work of relay centres in from of HPTs and LPTs throughout Jharkhand has become imperative.[3]

With the creation of new state of Jharkhand on 15th November, 2002, the responsibility of the first Doordarshan Kendra, i.e. DDK : Ranchi has increased many folds. With the modernization of technical facilities including inauguration and commissioning of Metro channel and uplinking facility, of a well equipped studio, duration of local transmission has increased from one hour to one and half hours in the benefit of the viewers under its coverage area.[4]

The SITE project meant for education and development of rural people in six states, namely, Rajasthan, Madhya Pradesh, Bihar, Andhra Pradesh, Karnataka and Orissa started in 1975-76. Under SITE continuity plan during 1976-82, six terrestrial transmitters were installed at different places and Muzaffarpur was one of them. When INSAT-1B was launched, beside SITE continuity project transmitters some more terrestrial transmitters with production facilities were installed during 1982 to produce 'Area Specific Programme' and Ranchi came under this scheme.

It was commissioned on priority basis in Ranchi on 25th September, 1984 to accelerate the socio-economic and cultural development of the people including tribals of this area.

Doordarshan Kendra : Ranchi is situated by the side of Ratu Road adjacent to Akashwani. It is accommodated in a building having a campus with an area of 2.75 acres. Presently, it accommodates one two storey transmitter building with an annexe.

The Kendra produces 'Area Specific Programmes' which is meant for a single Ethno-Cultural Zone and Jharkhand represents it in true sense. Programmes produced under it are for women, children, youth, agriculture, development, health, music and dance and industrial etc. All these programmes emphasizes tribals social, economic, culture, traditions etc., in particular and non-tribals in general.

Transmission Hours

Monday	:	5.30 pm - 7.15 pm
Tuesday	:	5.30 pm - 7.15 pm
Wednesday	:	5.30 pm - 7.15 pm
Thursday	:	5.30 pm - 7.15 pm
Friday	:	5.30 pm - 7.15 pm
Saturday	:	5.30 pm - 7.15 pm
Sunday	:	7.00 pm - 7.15 pm

Programme Composition

* **Format-Wise** (Average of 12 months)

(year '2000)

Terrestrial only

Programme	Minutes	Percentage
Current Affairs	109.0	9.5
Interview/Talk/Discussion	110.0	10.0
Documentary/Features	10.0	1.0
Poetry Recitation/Mushaira	13.0	1.0
Employment News/Information	0.0	0.0
Replies to Viewers letter	0.0	0.0
Sports	28.0	2.5
Music (Vocal/Inst/Folk etc.)	53.0	5.0

Contd...

Programme	Minutes	Percentage
Dance	51.0	5.0
Feature films/Tele films	0.0	0.0
Film songs	0.0	0.0
Plays/Serials/Skits	4.0	0.5
Quiz/Brain game/Prasna Manch	0.0	0.0
Children programme	27.0	2.0
Women programme (Rural and Urban)	29.0	3.0
Rural programme (Including Dev.)	523.0	48.0
Youth	32	3.0
Industrial workers	12	1.0
Tribals	31	3.0
Other language group	0	0.0
Adult education	0	0.0
Health/family welfare	18	2.0
School TV	0	0.0
Weekly programmes/ highlights/Saptahiki	0	0.0
Announcement/Slides/Fillers	38	3.5
Total Duration	1088	100

** **Source-wise** : (Average of 12 months)

(Year '2000)

DDK : Ranchi	1050	96.5
Outside Production (Indian and Foreign)	0	0.0
Announcement/Slides/Fillers	38	3.5
Total Duration	1088	100.0

* Format-Wise

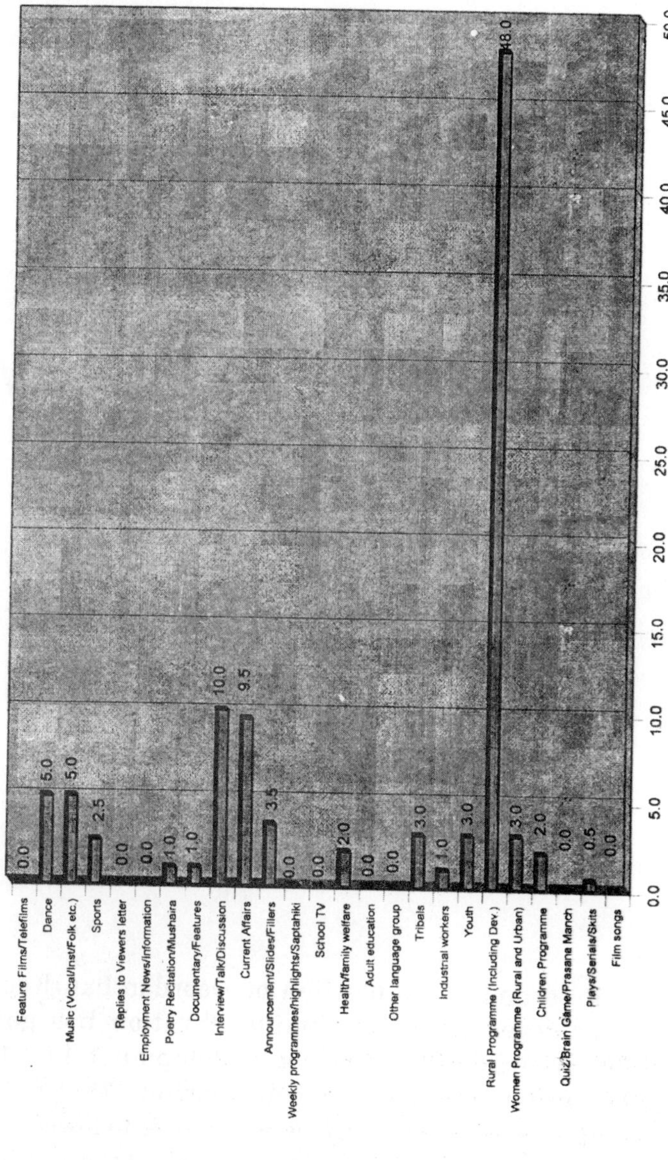
Feature Films/Telefilms 0.0
Dance 5.0
Music (Vocal/Inst/Folk etc.) 5.0
Sports 2.5
Replies to Viewers letter 0.0
Employment News/Information 0.0
Poetry Recitation/Mushaira 1.0
Documentary/Features 1.0
Interview/Talk/Discussion 10.0
Current Affairs 9.5
Announcement/Slides/Fillers 3.5
Weekly programmes/highlights/Saptahiki 0.0
School TV 0.0
Health/family welfare 2.0
Adult education 0.0
Other language group 0.0
Tribals 3.0
Industrial workers 1.0
Youth 3.0
Rural Programme (Including Dev.) 48.0
Women Programme (Rural and Urban) 3.0
Children Programme 2.0
Quiz/Brain Game/Prasana Manch 0.0
Plays/Serials/Skits 0.5
Film songs 0.0
0.0
5.0
10.0
15.0
20.0
25.0
30.0
35.0
40.0
45.0
50.0

**** Source-Wise**

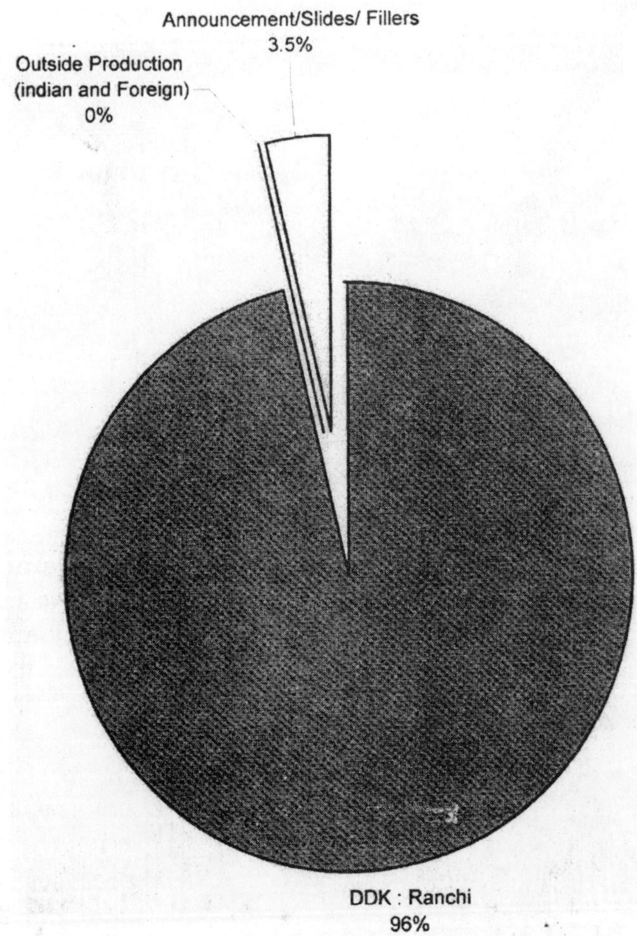

Programme composition of Doordarshan Kendra : Ranchi reveals that maximum duration has gone to rural programme including development i.e. 48.0% followed by interview/talk/discussion (10.0 %) then current affairs (9.5 %). Music and dance followed it with 5.0 % each in total programme share. Plays/serial/skits occupies only 0.5 % in total programme share.

The programmes are generally in Hindi but folk songs/dance and akhra programme are in local dialects of the area.

Significant Achievement

Some significant achievements of the Kendra is produced below :

- The Doordarshan-2 was installed to feed the viewers relay programmes specially entertainment programmes from Doordarshan Kendra, Ranchi.
- The uplinking facility has provided enough scope to establish inter-cultural correlation.
- Initially the viewers have had the opportunity of only 40 mts. Attachment but at present the transmission hour has been extended to 90 mts, to incorporate variety of other programmes as far as possible.
- Tribal art of Jharkhand specially wall painting, wood carving, palm leave products, bamboo made products etc. earned considerable popularity among the people coming from outside as well as to the areas adjacent to Jharkhand. But within the area, its exposure to the people of other culture was considerably at lower level. In this spectrum, Doordarshan, Ranchi has played valuable role to bring forward the specific cultural peculiarity to the common mass.
- Performing art is another spectrum where local talents hardly had the chance to be exposed before wide audience. It is the Doordarshan, Ranchi which has extended considerable impact in this field. New talents are thus being provided with enthusiasm to on their art performances towards further perfection as well as sophistication.
- Jharkhand is the treasure house of large variety medicinal plants. Local people do have strong faith

on it. To avert health hazards in remote places such plants very often play vital role. Doordarshan, Ranchi on the same line significantly interacted with the rural folk by channelising interesting programmes on medicinal plants covering disease types and corresponding available plants.

- In the awareness spectrum, it has earned considerable reputation. The programmes and the spots like leprosy, developmental programmes and spots on bank loan, safe drinking water etc. has found to percolate further beyond the urban sector, which has been revealed by a number of Audience Research Surveys.

References

1. Dr. S.Y. Quraishi, 'Preface', Doordarshan India 2002, Prasar Bharti, New Delhi.
2. Literature & Source : Doordarshan India 2002, Prasar Bharti, Broadcasting Corporation of India, Directorate General : Doordarshan (Audience Research Unit), Doordarshan Bhawan, New Delhi, July, 2002.
3. Anupam Swaroop, 'Foreword', Doordarshan in Jharkhand (Facts at a Glance '2002), Prasar Bharti, Audience Research Unit, Doordarshan Kendra : Ranchi
4. U.C. Mahapatra, 'Preface', Doordarshan in Jharkhand (Facts at a Glance '2002), Prasar Bharti. Audience Research Unit, Doordarshan Kendra : Ranchi.

3

Doordarshan :
A Microscopic Study (Methodology)

The study is concerned with that section of the Indian society which have been exploited in the past and which has remained under-privileged, backward and a deprived section of the traditional Indian society.

Hypothesis

The prime hypothesis of this study is to find out how the development of tribal people are influenced by the Doordarshan. Following are the hypothesis

(i) The viewing of Doordarshan is the part of life of tribal people.

(ii) Tribal people are more exposed to Doordarshan.

(iii) Tribal people are viewing more musical programmes as well as related to agriculture.

(iv) Doordarshan is bringing continuity and change among tribals and accelerate social, economic, occupational, political and cultural development.

(v) Doordarshan is bringing consciousness, modernity,

advanced education as well as health consciousness among the tribal people.

(vii) Doordarshan is bringing more consciousness among women for their freedom, position and status in the society.

(viii) Doordarshan correlates tribal and non-tribal culturally.

Descriptive Research Design

For the study of the impact of Doordarshan on tribals, a systematic method was needed and hence a study design or a research design was required to be prepared for the purpose. It is evident that different types of study designs are used in different situations and for the study of different problems. Thus selection of a particular study design is relevant to the nature of the problem and the objective of the study. As it helps in analyzing the impact of Doordarshan on tribals, it includes the analysis of their educational, social, economic, occupational, cultural and political development and their attitude, outlook, approaches, world-view, behaviour - patterns and forms of associations and interaction. It means that this study includes the analysis of the process of change and covers a wide range of problems. It refers to the analysis of existing social conditions and situations. In other words the study is more related to a descriptive analysis than to the exploration of causes and factors. Hence for the purpose of studying this problem a descriptive research design is more suitable. In view of these facts, the investigator was to draw a descriptive study design for studying the impact of Doordarshan on tribals of Chotanagpur (Jharkhand).

Research design is the plan of a piece of empirical research, specifying the manner in which data are to be collected and analysed in order to test hypotheses derived from theory, or to develop insights into the problem being investigated. It combines relevance to the problem with economy in procedure. The design stage is the most crucial phase of the research process. A particular design may involve experiment, social survey, participant observation, other methods, or a combination of more than one procedure.

After taking a decision in respect of the study design, the investigator was faced with the task of taking a decision about the techniques of data collection to be applied in the present study.

Interview Schedule

To use interview schedule is more convenient in data collection. The major difficulty in using questionnaire technique is concerned with the illiteracy of some viewers. Schedule contains certain questions and blank tables in which the information required is filled up by the interviewers, the field workers or the investigator as the case may be. Some information can be collected through questions while other can be elicited with the help of the tables. This is a device for collecting data.

Schedule is a list of questions. Through these questions the data or the requisite information is collected. It is a standardized device or tool of observation or interview for collecting data in a objective manner. In this method, the interviewer puts certain questions and the viewer furnishes certain answers and the interviewer records them as the answers are furnished. It has the following purposes

(i) To collect information or data in an objective manner.

(ii) To help in memory

(iii) To facilitate and help in the work of tabulation and analysis of the data.

With the help of schedule the investigator, who himself acts as an interviewer or if the project is large sends some one else to act as an interviewer, collects the relevant and requisite information about a particular problem in an objective manner.

It is not possible for the interviewer to keep in mind or memories, all the information that he has collected from different respondents. If no standardized tool is available he might put different question to different viewer and thereby get confused when he has to analyse and tabulate the data. Schedule acts as a memory tickler.

The third purpose is to table and analyse the data collected in a homogenous manner.

Schedule that are used in social research have been classified by various social scientists and sociologists. Observation schedule are used for observation and are known as 'observation schedule'. They contain certain specific topics about which the interviewer has to collect information or data. Such a schedule contains pointed questions in regard to specific topics. Normally these types of schedules have two fold purposes, on one hand, the interviewer observes the phenomena and on the other hand he himself makes certain observations. Apart from it he sometimes puts certain questions to the viewer and collects information on the basis of the observation of the viewer.

Rating schedule – this type of schedule is used in the cases in which on the basis of the schedule, certain evaluation or rating is to be done. This schedule is helpful in determining the factors that are responsible for shaping of a particular event or phenomena. In this type of schedule, different scales, ranks or measures are constructed and on the basis of them evaluation or rating is done.

Institutional survey schedule – this type of schedule is used for studying the different problems of the institutions. P.V.Young has defined that 'these schedules are designed to add in visualizing to the problems faced by or the situation inherent in given institution.'

Document schedule – In this type of schedule, the documents are used, or the studies based on documents. This type of schedule is generally used for writing the history or the documents. On the basis of the available material, certain questions are asked and on the basis of the answers the life history is written. For successful use of this method it is necessary that more than required material about the life history and the documents should be available. This type of schedule, as we have already seen, is generally used for recording data from written documents like autobiography, diary, case history on final records of the government etc. It is a good method for collecting primary data or preparing source list.

Interview schedule – This type of schedule is normally used for testing and evaluating the collected data and also for collection of the supplementary data. Generally it is used in interviews. There are certain standardized questions that are asked by the interviewer and he has to fill in the information received in the tables.

Interview schedule is quite scientific and adequate. Thus, the investigator has uses this type of schedule for the information and data collection in the present study.

Sampling

Most social research inquiries, except censuses and some type of official statistics, are based on cases selected from a larger population, so the question arises of how representative the cases studied are of the population from which they are drawn. The statistical theory of sampling, itself based on probability theory, provides a rigorous means of checking on representativeness, provided that certain conditions are met.

Probability or random sampling requires the selection of units from a population in such a way that each unit has a known and non-zero chance of selection. Selection is usually made from a list of the population, if it is available, such as the register of electors for a national survey; this list is known as the sampling-frame. Selection uses either a table of random numbers, or a random starting point and then units selected at fixed intervals according to the proportion of the population being sampled (the sampling fraction). The latter procedure is known as systematic sampling.

The resulting list of units selected is known as the sample. It may be a list of individuals, but it could equally well be a list of institutions, groups, or other collectivity, depending on the subject of research. Selection according to stric principles of randomness, as defined above, is essential if correct statistical inferences are to be made from the sample to the population. Haphazard selection of units, however carried out, cannot be random in the statistical sense.

Different types of sample design are possible.

(i) **Multi-stage samples** : in national surveys, regions or counties may be sampled at the first stage; cities, towns or their subdivisions sampled within first-stage units at the second stage; and households or individuals sampled within second stage units at the third stage. This achieves considerable economies in interviewing.

(ii) **Multi-phase sampling** : drawing a general sample as a first step, then among those selected, identifying those with certain specified characteristics for detailed interviewing (e.g. in a study of fertility in women of child-bearing age). This type of design may be used where no convenient sampling frame of a special group exists.

Stratification in sampling takes account of factors known to be likely to affect the results of a survey (e.g. regional, social class differences, age, sex etc.). Prior to the sample being selected, the sampling frame is recorded according to the factors by which the sample is stratified. Thus in the sample, the proportion of the sample drawn from a given stratum is known, and can be varied if the stratum is small.

Provided that random sampling is used, then reliable estimates may be made from the sample to the population from which it is drawn, including the calculation of confidence intervals and the sampling error.

Sample size is very often determined by practical considerations such as time and money. No rules exist for determining the size of sample, though in deciding upon a target sample size, account should be taken of the precision of the results sought (what margin of sampling error is tolerable) and the type of multivariate analysis to be performed upon the data. Sample size, too, must take account of the response rate.

The size of the sample will not usually correspond to the number of interviews eventually completed. The number of completed interviews as a proportion of the original sample is the completion rate or response rate. Non-response in survey sampling may be due to individuals who are not-at-home (due to being at work, always out, in hospital, on holiday, dead etc) and those who refuse to participate in a survey (for whatever reason). In practice these shade into one another, and there are conditions in between (those who are too young or too old to be interviewed, don't understand the interviewer etc). The achieved sample is likely to be smaller than the original sample selected. Completion rates for mail surveys are considerably lower than those for personal interview surveys.

These procedure rest upon probablity theory and the use of the central limit theorem to make inferences from a sample to a population, using the properties of the normal distribution. Some forms of sampling do not use random selection, in which case none of the foregoing applies. Quota sampling, widely used in market research, gives interviewers quotas of particular types of people to be interviewed (e.g. by combinations of age, sex, and social class) but leaves it to the interviewer to make the selection of individuals to be approached. This can result in bias in selection, but it also means that sampling errors cannot be calculated, not a completion rate worked out. Other types of sampling (e.g. snowball sampling) do not even possess the controls provided by the use of quotas, and are only recommended in sampling rare populations to which it is difficult to gain access.

The use of random sampling, particularly in social survey research, gives the social scientist an extremely powerful means of meeting the criterion of representativeness in research. Its use, particularly in large-scale surveys, is however costly and labour-intensive.[1]

The investigator has applied purposive sampling method for the representative samples in the present study. Purposive sampling method is scientific, representative and adequate. There is specific purpose or objective. The investigator, while making purposive selection, should keep himself free from prejudices and bias. The investigator keeping in the view the knowledge and the object or the purpose, selects only those samples that are relevant and representative of the entire population or universe. Purposive sampling method can be successful only if the investigator has full knowledge about the nature of the universe and other statistical measurement about it.

In this method if prejudices and bias have been avoided even a small sample can be representative and if the sample has been selected cautiously the purpose of the research is fulfilled without any botheration.

In the present study the universe under study is tribal people of Chotanagpur, who is living and working in Ranchi town. For the study, 200 tribals people have been selected as sample.

Observation

In the field of social science research, observation was probably the oldest method of investigation. Observation starts with curiosity which is natural for every man and child. If observation is conducted without gaining and without keeping object in view it more or les meaningless and has no higher objective. When without this, observation is carried out, with an objective in view, it leads to development of an organized branch of knowledge.

In this method the sense organs particularly eye, ear, voice etc. are used. Greater use is made of eye. In this method through direct contact with environment, the data is collected. The main purpose of this method is to collect the primary data. The investigator first of all observes things and then collects data. The investigator or the researcher himself comes in contact with the phenomena or the field of study. Because of this relationship is established between the investigator and the viewers, this relationship is helpful in order to make the work more scientific. It is a classical scientific method through which data about the social problems are collected. Infact it is a dependable method for collection of detailed data from a wide field.

The investigator has applied non-participant observation method in the present work. In this method of observation, the observer is present in the group, but he does not participate in their activities. Non-participant observation method has an important place or utility in the social research.

On the basis of the tools of data collection, the data thus obtained from field have been given statistical treatment in the following chapters.

References

1. Michel Mann, 'Sociology', 1983.

4

Doordarshan :
An Overview of the Viewers

The present chapter is related with an overview of the viewers under this study. The data are presented in classified and tabulated manner for an interpretative and systematic analysis.

Table – 1.1

Age Groupings

Age Groups	Number	Percentage
Below 25	40	20.0
26-35	60	30.0
36-45	70	35.0
46 and above	30	15.0
Total	200	100.0

The table presents the age composition of the sample under study. It is found from the table that the viewers belong to different age ranges from below 25 years to 46 and above. It is evident from the above table that 35.0 percent of the viewers are from the age group of 36-45 years. 30.0 percent of the viewers are from the age group of 26-35 years. 20.0 percent of the viewers are from the age group of below 25 years and 15.0 percent of the viewers are from the age group of 46 and above years.

Table – 1.2

Sex

Sex	Number	Percentage
Male	100	50.0
Felame	100	50.0
Total	200	100.0

The table 1.2 presents the classification of the viewers on the basis of sex. It is evident from the table that 50 percent of the viewers are male whereas rest 50 percent of the total viewers are female. It is important to note here that tribal male and female both are residing and working in Ranchi town.

Table – 1.3

Upbringing and Background

Background	Number	Percentage
Rural	160	80.0
Urban	40	20.0
Total	200	100.0

The table 1.3 shows that 80 percent of the total viewers are from rural background whereas only 20 percent of the total viewers are from urban background. It is important to note that the place of birth and the environment in which a tribe spends his/her impressionable years play an important part in determining his-her attitude towards life and the pattern of his/her behaviour.

Table – 1.4

Eductional Qualification

Qualification	Number	Percentage
Illiterate	30	15.0
Up to secondary	80	40.0
Matriculation	40	20.0
Up to graduation	35	17.5
Post-graduation	10	5.0
Above Post-graduation	5	2.5
Total	200	100.0

It is clear from the table 1.4 that 15 percent of the total viewers are illiterate whereas 40 percent of the viewers are educated up to secondary level. 20 percent of the viewers are educated up to matriculation level, 17.5 percent of the viewers are educated up to graduation level. 5 percent of the total viewers are educated up to post-graduation level and only 2.5 percent of the total viewers are educated up to above post-graduation level. It is evident from the above table that still the tribal people (15%) are illiterate but they are working and earning and have some other useful qualifications. It is also evident from the table that a few percent of tribal people are educated above post-graduation level.

Table – 1.5

Religion

Religion	Number	Percentage
Sarna	110	55.0
Christianity	90	45.0
Total	200	100.0

The table presents the classification of the viewers on the basis of religion. It is evident from the table that 55 percent of the total viewers belong to Sarna religion (very near to Hindu) whereas 45 percent of the total viewers belong to Christianity. It is important to note here that all viewers (45%) are converted Christians.

Table – 1.6

Marital Status

Marital Status	Number	Percent
Unmarried	70	35.0
Married	125	62.5
Widow/Divorced	5	2.5
Total	200	100.0

It is evident from the table 1.6 that 62.5 percent of the total viewers are married whereas 35 percent of the viewers are unmarried. Only 2.5 percent of the viewers are widow or divorced.

Table – 1.7

Occupation

Occupation	Number	Percentage
Service	60	30.0
Agriculture	20	10.0

Self Business	20	10.0
Labourer	50	25.0
Others	50	25.0
Total	200	100.0

The Table 1.7 presents the classification of viewers on the basis of occupation. The table shows that 30 percent of the total viewers are in service, 10 percent of the viewers are engaged in agriculture, 10 percent of the viewers are doing self-business and 25 percent of the viewers studying or doing work for house-hold affairs whereas 25 percent of the total viewers are working as labourers.

It is important to note here that agriculture is the main work and earning of the tribals in Jharkhand. There is so many village markets in this state. It is also important to note here that building construction is one of the main profession of the tribal people as Mistri or Reza.

Table – 1.8

Income

Income	Number	Percentage
Below 2000/-	60	30.0
2001-4000/-	50	25.0
4001-6000/-	40	20.0
6001-8000/-	25	12.5
8001-10000/-	15	7.5
Above 10000/-	10	5.0
Total	200	100.0

The table 1.8 clearly shows that 30 percent of the total viewers are earning below 2000/- per month. The income of 25 percent of the viewers are 2001 to 4000/- per month, 20 percent of the viewers are earning 4001 to 6000/- per month, 12.5 percent of the viewers are earning 6001 to 8000/- per month, whereas 7.5 percent of the viewers are earning 8001 to 10000/- per month. The earning of only 5 percent of the viewers are above 10000/- per month. It is important to note that it consists both personal and family income per month. It means that a majority of 55 percent of the viewers are still earning only up to 4000/- per month. Economic condition is not at all satisfactory. It is important to note here that tribal people are still exploited by the exploiters.

Table – 1.9

Family Types

Family Types	Number	Percentage
Joint family	70	35.0
Nuclear family	130	65.0
Total	200	100.0

Table 1.9 presents the classification of the viewers on the basis of the types of family they live in. It is found from the table that 65 percent of the total viewers are living in nuclear families whereas 35 percent of the viewers are living in joint families. It is important that in spite of living and working in an urban area and having education to some extent, a considerable percentage of viewers still live in joint family.

Table – 1.10

Family Size

Family Size	Number	Percent
Below 4 members	30	15.0
5-7 members	60	30.0

8-10 members	70	35.0
11-13 members	30	15.0
Above 13 members	10	5.0
Total	200	100.0

The table 1.10 presents the classification of viewers on the basis of family size. It is evident from the table that 15 percent of the total viewers are living with, below 4 members in his family whereas 30 percent of the viewers are living with 5 to 7 members in his family. 35 percent of the viewers are living with 8 to 10 members in his family whereas 15 percent of the viewers are living with 11 to 13 members in his family. Only 5 percent of the viewers are living with above 13 members in his family.

Table – 1.11

Ownership of Building

Building	Number	Percentage
Own	105	55.0
Rented	95	45.0
Total	200	100.0

The Table 1.11 presents the classification of the viewers on the basis of ownership of building. It is evident from the table that 55 percent of the total viewers has own building whereas 45 percent of the viewers live in rented building. It is important to note that the types of building whether it is 'kachcha, pakka, jhopri and tin ka' all are included in the building. It is also important to note that some of the viewers are working in town but coming from 'dehat' and there they have own building or 'makan or jhopri or kachcha ka makan or pakka ka building. Some of the viewers have their own building in the urban area.

Table – 1.12

Types of Tribals

Name	Number	Percentage
Oraon	60	30.0
Munda	60	30.0
Santhal	40	20.0
Ho	20	10.0
Kharia	10	5.0
others	10	5.0
Total	200	100.0

The table 1.12 presents the classification of viewers on the basis of different types of tribe. It is evident from the table that 30 percent of the total viewers are Oraon tribe, 30 percent of them are Munda tribe, 20 percent of the viewers are Santhal tribe, 10 percent of them are Ho tribe, 5 percent of the viewers are from Kharia tribe and 5 percent of these tribes belongs to 'others' category.

5

Doordarshan and Other Mass Media

Exposure to the mass media is an important variable in large-scale directed social change, and modernization in developing political life of a transitional society via 'the minds and hearts of its people'. It teaches people by depicting few and strange situations and familiarise them with a range of opinions among which they choose. Lerner states that "increasingly, in the villages and home of the world, the mass media are bringing 'strange new world' into the traditional environment of rural people". The nature and scope of the mass media differs from one country to another. In the communication process in transitional societies, the urban villages levels are not closely integrated. In less developed countries, it reaches only to smaller audiences, such as university students, members of professions, the middle class, and urban dwellers. This is due to the availability, and the degree of government control. Communication can be direct or indirect, face to face contact versus the impersonal channels. Recent years have shown a tremendous growth in mass media techniques. By using these new techniques such as radio and television, the governments of developing countries are reaching larger audiences.

In this chapter certain questions were asked from the viewers to find out the impact of Doordarshan in particular and other media of mass communication in general and their degree of exposure to the media of mass communication.

Table – 2.1
TV viewing

Age group	N	TV Viewing			
		Yes	%	No	%
Below 25	40	40	100.0	–	–
26–35	60	60	100.0	–	–
36–45	70	70	100.0	–	–
46 and above	30	30	100.0	–	–
Total	200	200	100.0	–	–

The table 2.1 presents the classification of viewers on the basis of TV viewing. For this, age variable are used. It is evident fom the table that 100 percent of the viewers replied in positive. Not even a single viewer replied in negative. It is important to note that due to low income some of the viewers are still without a set of television but they used to see television. Some of the viewers are enjoying television programme at his/her employer's shop or resident. It is also important to note that television is the most popular media among the viewers.

Table – 2.2

TV viewing : Frequency

Age groups	N	Regularly		A number of times a week		At least once a week		Ocassionally	
		N	%	N	%	N	%	N	%
Below 25	40	5	12.5	10	25.0	11	27.5	14	35.0
26–35	60	10	16.6	15	25.0	17	28.3	18	30.0
36–45	70	13	18.5	15	21.4	19	27.1	23	32.8
46 and above	30	14	46.6	9	30.0	5	16.6	2	6.6
Total	200	42	21.0	49	24.5	52	26.0	57	28.5

The above table presents the classification of viewers on the basis of frequency of TV viewing. For this, age variable are used. It evident from the table that 12.5 percent of the viewers are viewing TV regularly, 25 percent of the viewers are viewing TV a number of times a week, 27.5 percent of the viewers are viewing TV at least once a week and 35 percent of the viewers are viewing TV occasionally in the age group category of below 25. 16.6 percent of the viewers are viewing TV regularly, 25 percent of the viewers are viewing TV a number of times a week, 28.3 percent of the viewers are viewing TV at least once a week and 30 percent of the viewers are viewing TV occasionally in the age group category of 26–35. 18.5 percent of the viewers are viewing TV regularly, 21.4 percent of the viewers are viewing TV a number of times a week, 27.1 percent of the viewers are viewing TV at least once a week and 32.8 percent of the viewers are viewing TV occasionally in the age group category of 36–45. 46.6 percent of the viewers are viewing TV regularly, 30 percent of the viewers are viewing TV a number of times a week, 16.6 percent of the viewers are viewing

TV at least once a week and 6.6 percent of the viewers are viewing TV occasionally in the age group category of 46 and above.

21 percent of the total viewers are viewing TV regularly, 24.5 percent of the total viewers are viewing TV a number of times a week, 26 percent of the total viewers are viewing TV at least once a week and 28.5 percent of the total viewers are viewing TV occasionally.

Table – 2.3

Viewing Doordarshan and Other Satellite/Cable Channels

Age groups	N	Doordarshan				Other Channels			
		Yes	%	No	%	Yes	%	No	%
Below 25	40	40	100.0	–	–	24	60.0	16	40.0
26–35	60	60	100.0	–	–	33	55.0	27	45.0
36–45	70	70	100.0	–	–	28	40.0	42	60.0
46 and above	30	30	100.0	–	–	6	20.0	24	80.0
Total	200	200	100.0	–	–	91	45.5	109	54.5

The above table presents the classification of the viewers on the basis of viewing Doordarshan and other channels. It is evident from the table that 100 percent of the viewers replied in positive as far as Doordarshan is concerned. Not even a single viewer replied in negative. It is evident from the table that 45.5 percent of the total viewers are viewing other cable channels also. 54.5 percent of the total viewers are not enjoying other cable channels. 60 percent of the viewer in the category of below 25, 55 percent of the viewers in the category of 26–35, 40 percent of the viewers in the category o 36–45 and 20 percent of the viewers in the category of 46 and above are enjoying other cable channels also. It is important to note that they are viewing Doordarshan without cost.

Table – 2.4

Doordarshan Programme Viewing (Mainly)

Age groups	N	Current Affairs		Films/ Tele/Doc Films		Music/ Dance/ Cultural		Rural		Others	
		N	%	N	%	N	%	N	%	N	%
Below 25	40	7	17.5	15	37.5	10	25.0	3	7.5	5	12.5
26–35	60	10	16.6	22	36.6	15	25.0	5	8.3	8	13.3
36–45	70	15	21.4	20	28.5	17	24.2	10	14.2	8	11.4
46 and above	30	2	6.6	3	10.0	7	23.3	16	53.3	2	6.6
Total	200	34	17.0	60	30.0	49	24.5	34	17.0	23	11.5

The table 2.4 shows that 17 percent of the total viewers are viewing mainly the programme related to current affairs, 30 percent of the total viewers are viewing mainly films whether it is film or tele film or documentary film. 24.5 percent of the total viewers are viewing mainly the programme of music or dance or other culture programmes. 17 percent of the total viewers are mainly viewing rural programmes and 11.5 percent of the total viewers are mainly viewing the other programmes of Doordarshan, such as children programme, women programme, the programme of youth and tribals, health and family welfare and the programme of regional concern.

Table – 2.5

Effects of Doordarshan

Age groups	N	Doordarshan					
		Good	%	Bad	%	Both	%
Below 25	40	30	75.0	2	5.0	8	20.0
26–35	60	35	58.3	5	8.3	20	33.3

36–45	70	50	71.4	6	8.5	14	20.0
46 and above	30	25	83.3	1	3.3	4	13.3
Total	200	140	70.0	14	7.0	46	23.0

It is evident from the table 2.5 that according to 75 percent of the viewers, the effects of Doordarshan are good, according to 5 percent of the viewers, the effects are bad and according to 20 percent of viewers, the effects are both good and bad in the age group category of below 25. According to 58.3 percent of the viewers, the effects are good, according to 8.3 percent of the viewers, the effects are bad, according to 33.3 percent of the viewers, the effects are both good and bad in the age group category of 26–35. According to 71.4 percent of the viewers, the effects are good, according to 8.5 percent of the viewers, the effects are bad and according to 20 percent of the viewers, the effects are both good and bad in the age group category of 36–45. According to 83.3 percent of the viewers, the effects are good, according to 3.3 percent of the viewers, the effects are bad and 13.3 percent of the viewers, the effects are both good and bad in the age group category of 46 and above.

It is evident from the table that 70 percent of the total viewers hold the view that Doordarshan produces good effects, 23 percent of the total viewers hold the view that Doordarshan produces both good and bad effects and only 7 percent of the total viewers hold the view that Doordarshan produces bad effects.

It is important to note that a majority of the viewers hold the view that Doordarshan not only provides much needed entertainment to the rural and urban people but also exposes them to social, economic, political, religious and cultural themes and consciousness. The documentaries fulfill a much desired need for information. The viewers still remember 'Ramayana', 'Mahabharat', 'Rajani', etc.

Table – 2.6

Effects of Other Satellite/Cable Channels

Age groups	N	Other Cable Channels					
		Good	%	Bad	%	Both	%
Below 25	40	8	20.0	30	75.0	2	5.0
26–35	60	7	11.6	33	55.0	20	33.3
36–45	70	10	14.2	46	65.7	14	20.0
46 and above	30	2	6.6	24	80.0	4	13.3
Total	200	27	13.5	133	66.5	40	20.0

It is evident from the table 2.6 that according to 20 percent of the viewers, the effects of other cable channels are good whereas according to 75 percent of the viewers, the effects are bad whereas 5 percent of the viewers hold the view that the effects of other cable channels are both good and bad in the age group category of below 25 years. According to 11.6 percent of the viewers, the effects are good whereas 55 percent of the viewers hold the view that the effects of other cable channels are bad. 33.3 percent of the viewers hold the view that the effects are both good and bad in the age group of 26–35 years. 14.2 percent of the viewers hold the view that the effects are good whereas a majority of 65.7 percent of the viewers hold the view that the effects of other cable channels are bad and 20 percent of the viewers hold the view that the effects are both good and bad in the age group of 36–45 years. Only 6.6 percent of the viewers hold the view that the effects of other cable channels are good whereas a majority of 80 percent of the viewers hold the view that the effects of other cable channels are bad and 13.3 percent of the viewers hold the view that the effects of other cable channels are both good and bad in the age group category of 46 and above years.

It is also evident from the table that a majority of 66.5 percent of the total viewers hold the view that the effects of other cable channels are bad whereas only 13.5 percent of the viewers hold the view that the effects are good and 20 percent of the viewers hold the view that the effects of other cable channels are both good and bad.

Table – 2.7

Cinema Viewing

Age groups	N	Yes	%	No	%
Below 25	40	24	60.0	16	40.0
26–35	60	33	55.0	27	45.0
35–45	70	40	57.1	30	42.8
46 and above	30	7	23.3	23	76.6
Total	200	104	52.0	96	48.0

It is evident from the table 2.7 that 60 percent of the total viewers are viewing cinema whereas 40 percent of the total viewers are not viewing cinema in the age group category of below 25. Out of total viewers 55 percent are viewing cinema whereas 45 percent of the total viewers are not viewing cinema in the age group category of 26–35. 57.1 percent of the total viewers are viewing cinema whereas 42.8 percent of the total viewers are not viewing cinema in age group category of 36–45 and 23.3 percent of the total viewers are viewing cinema whereas 76.6 percent of the total viewers are not viewing cinema in the age groups category of 46 and above.

It is evident from the table that 52 percent of the total viewers are viewing cinema whereas 48 percent of the total viewers are not viewing cinema.

Table – 2.8

Cinema Viewing : Frequency

Age groups	N	Once a week		Once a month		Occasion-ally	
	Yes	N	%	N	%	N	%
Below	24	4	16.6	5	20.8	15	62.5
26–35	33	3	9.0	10	30.3	20	60.6
36–45	40	2	5.0	10	25.0	28	70.0
46 and above	7	–	–	1	14.2	6	85.7
Total	104	9	8.6	26	25.0	69	66.3

It is evident from the table 2.8 that 16.6 percent of the viewers are viewing cinema once a week whereas 20.8 percent of the viewers are viewing cinema once a month and a majority of 62.5 percent of the viewers are viewing cinema occasionally in the age group of below 25 years. 9 percent of the viewers are viewing cinema once a week whereas 30.3 percent of the viewers are viewing cinema once a month and a majority of 60.6 percent of the viewers are viewing cinema occasionally in the age group of 26–35 years. 5 percent of the viewers are viewing cinema once a week whereas 25 percent of the viewers are viewing cinema once a month and a majority of 70 percent of the viewers are viewing cinema occasionally in the age group of 36–45 years. A majority of 85.7 percent of the viewers are viewing cinema occasionally whereas only 14.2 percent of the viewers are viewing cinema once a month in the age group category of 46 and above years. It is important to note that not even a single viewer in this category is viewing cinema once a week.

It is also evident from the table that a majority of 66.3 percents of the total viewers are viewing cinema occasionally whereas 25 percent of the total viewers are viewing cinema once a month and only 8.6 percent of the total viewers are viewing cinema once a week.

It is important to note here that only 104 (52%) out of 200 viewers replied that they are viewing cinema, therefore the total N is 104 in this table.

Table – 2.9

Effects of Cinema

Age groups	N	Cinema					
		Good	%	Bad	%	Both	%
Below 25	40	10	25.0	20	50.0	10	25.0
26–35	60	12	20.0	32	53.3	16	26.6
36–45	70	16	22.8	30	42.8	24	34.2
46 and above	30	2	6.6	20	66.6	8	26.6
Total	200	40	20.0	102	51.0	58	29.0

It is evident from the table 2.9 that 25 percent of the viewers hold the view that the effects of cinema are good whereas a majority of 50 percent of the viewers hold the view that the effects are bad and 25 percent of the viewers hold the view that the effects of cinema are both good and bad in the age group category of below 25 years. According to 20 percent of the viewers, the effects of cinema are good whereas a majority of 53.3 percent of the viewers hold the view that the effects of cinema are bad and according to 26.6 percent of the viewers, the effects of cinema are both good and bad in the age group category of 26–35 years. 22.8

percent of the viewers hold the view that the effects of cinema are good whereas 42.8 percent of the viewers hold the view that the effects of cinema are bad and 34.2 percent of the viewers hold the view that the effects of cinema are both good and bad in the age group category of 36–45 years. A majority of 66.6 percent of the viewers hold the view that the effects of cinema are bad whereas only 2 percent of the viewers hold the view that the effects are bad and 26.6 percent of the viewers hold the view that the effects of cinema are both good and bad in the age group category of 46 and above years.

It is also evident from the table that a majority of 51 percent of the total viewers hold the view that the effects of cinema are bad whereas 20 percent of the total viewers hold the view that the effects of cinema are good and 29 percent of the total viewers hold the view that the effects of cinema are both good and bad in the age group category of 46 and above years.

Table – 2.10

Newspaper Reading

Age Group	N	Newspaper Reading			
		Yes	%	No	%
Below 25	40	25	62.5	15	37.5
26–35	60	32	53.3	28	46.6
36–45	70	36	51.4	34	48.5
46 and above	30	5	16.6	25	83.3
Total	200	98	49.0	102	51.0

The table 2.10 show that 62.5 percent of the viewers are reading newspaper whereas 37.5 percent of the viewers are not reading newspaper in the age group category of below 25 years. 53.3 percent of the viewers are reading newspaper whereas 46.6 percent of the viewers are not reading newspaper in the age group category of 26–35 years. 51.4 percent of the viewers are reading newspaper whereas 48.5 percent of the viewers are not reading newspaper in the age group category of 36–45 years. 16.6 percent of the viewers are reading newspaper whereas 83.3 percent of the viewers are not reading newspaper in the age group category of 46 and above years.

It is also evident from the table that 49 percent of the total viewers are reading newspaper whereas 51 percent of the total viewers are not reading newspaper.

Table – 2.11

Newspaper Reading : Frequency

Age groups	N	Newspaper Reading			
	Yes	Regularly	%	Occasionally	%
Below 25	25	14	56.0	11	44.0
26–35	32	18	56.2	14	43.7
36–45	36	20	55.5	16	44.4
46 and above	5	1	20.0	4	80.0
Total	98	53	54.0	45	45.9

It is evident from the table 2.11 that 56 percent of the viewers are reading newspaper regularly whereas 44 percent of the viewers are reading newspaper occasionally in the age group category of below 25 years. 56.2 percent of the viewers are reading newspaper regularly. Whereas 43.7 percent of the viewers are reading newspaper occasionally in the age group category of 26–35 years. 55.5 percent of the viewers are reading newspaper regularly whereas 44.4 percent of the viewers are reading newspaper occasionally in the age group category of 36–45 years. 20 percent of the viewers are reading newspaper regularly whereas 80 percent of the viewers are reading newspaper occasionally in the age group category of 46 and above years.

It is also evident from the table that 54 percent of the total viewers are reading newspaper regularly whereas 45.9 percent of the total viewers are reading newspaper occasionally. It is important to note here that only 98 (49%) viewers are reading newspaper, therefore the total N is 98 = 100 %

Table – 2.12

Effects of Newspaper

Age groups	N	Newspaper : Effects					
		Good	%	Bad	%	Both	%
Below 25	40	15	37.5	5	12.5	20	50.0
26–35	60	24	40.0	6	10.0	30	50.0
36–45	70	25	35.7	5	7.1	40	57.1
46 and above	30	12	40.0	3	10.0	15	50.0
Total	200	76	38.0	19	9.5	105	52.5

The table 2.12 reflect that 37.5 percent of the viewers hold the view that the effects of newspaper are good whereas 12.5 percent of the viewers hold the view that the effects of newspaper are bad and a majority of 50 percent of the viewers hold the view that the effects of newspaper are both good and bad in the age category of below 25 years. 40 percent of the viewers hold the view that the effects of newspaper are good whereas 10 percent of the viewers hold the view that the effects of newspaper are bad and a majority of 50 percent of the viewers hold the view that the effects of newspaper are both good and bad in the age group category of 26–35 years. 35.7 percent of the viewers hold the view that the effects of newspaper are good whereas 7.1 percent of the viewers hold the view that the effects of newspaper are bad and a majority of 57.1 percent of the viewers hold the view that the effects of newspaper are both good and bad in the age group category of 36–45 years. 40 percent of the viewers hold the view that the effects of newspaper are good whereas 10 percent of the viewers hold the view that the effects of newspaper are bad and a majority of 50 percent of the viewers hold the view that the effects of newspaper are both good and bad in the age group of 46 and above years.

It is also evident from the table that 38 percent of the total viewers hold the view that the effects of newspaper are good whereas 9.5 percent of the total viewers hold the view that the effects of newspaper are bad and a majority of 52.5 percent of the viewers hold the view that the effects of newspaper are both good and bad.

Table – 2.13

Radio Listening

Age groups	N	Radio Listening			
		Yes	%	No	%
Below 25	40	38	95.0	2	5.0
26–35	60	58	96.6	2	3.3
36–45	70	65	92.8	5	7.1
46 and above	30	29	96.6	1	3.3
Total	200	190	95.0	10	5.0

It is evident from the table 2.13 that 95 percent of the viewers are listening radio whereas only 5 percent of the viewers are not listening radio in the age group category of below 25 years. 96.6 percent of the viewers are listening radio whereas only 3.3 percent of the viewers are not listening radio in the age group category of 26–35 years. 92.8 percent of the viewers are listening radio whereas only 7.1 percent of the viewers are not listening radio programmes. 96.6 percent of the viewers are listening radio programmes whereas only 3.3 percent of the viewers are not listening radio programmes in the age group of 46 and above years.

It is also evident from the table that 95 percent of the total viewers are listening radio programmes whereas only 5 percent of the total viewers are not listening radio programmes.

Table – 2.14

Effects of Radio Programmes

Age groups	N	Radio Programme : Effects					
		Good	%	Bad	%	Both	%
Below 25	40	30	75.0	1	2.5	9	22.5
26–35	60	40	66.6	2	3.3	18	30.0
36–45	70	50	71.4	3	4.2	17	24.2
46 and above	30	20	66.6	2	6.6	8	26.6
Total	200	140	70.0	8	4.0	52	26.0

The table 2.14 presents the effects of radio programmes among other mass media. It is evident from the table that 75 percent of the viewers hold the view that the effects of radio programme are good whereas 2.5 percent of the viewers hold the view that the effects of radio programme are bad and 22.5 percent of the viewers hold the view that the effects of radio programme are both good and bad in the age group category of below 25 years. 66.6 percent of the viewers hold the view that the effects of radio programme are good whereas only 3.3 percent of the viewers hold the view that the effects of radio programme are bad and 30 percent of the viewers hold the view that the effects of radio programme are both good and bad in the age group of 26–35 years. A majority of 71.4 percent of the viewers hold the view that the effects of radio programme are good whereas only 4.2 percent of the viewers hold the view that the effects of radio programme are bad and 24.2 percent of the viewers hold the view that the effects of radio programme are both good and bad in the age group category of 36–45 years. 66.6 percent of the viewers hold the view that the effects of radio programme are good whereas 6.6 percent of the viewers hold the view that the effects of radio programme are bad and 26.6 percent of the viewers hold the view that the effects of radio programme are both good and bad in the age group category of 46 and above years.

It is evident from the table that a majority of 70 percent of the total viewers hold the view that the effects of radio programme are good whereas only 4 percent of the total viewers hold the view that the effects of radio programme are bad and 26 percent of the total viewers hold the view that the effects are both good and bad.

Table – 2.15

Magazine Reading

Age groups	N	Magazine Reading			
		Yes	%	No	%
Below 25	40	10	25.0	30	75.0
26–35	60	20	33.3	40	66.6
36–45	70	15	21.4	55	78.5
46 and above	30	3	10.0	27	90.0
Total	200	48	24.0	152	76.0

The table 2.15 clearly indicate that 25 percent of the viewers are reading magazines whereas 75 percent of the viewers are not reading magazines in the age group of below 25 years. 33.3 percent of the viewers are reading magazines whereas 66.6 percent of the viewers are not reading magazines in the age group of 26–35 years. 21.4 percent of the viewers are reading magazines whereas 78.5 percent of the viewers are not reading magazines in the age group of 36–45 years. Only 10 percent of the viewers are reading magazines whereas 99 percent of the viewers are not reading magazines in the age group of 46 and above years.

It is also evident from the table that 24 percent of the total viewers are reading magazines whereas a majority of 76 percent of the total viewers are not reading magazines.

Table – 2.16

Magazine Reading : Effects

Age groups	N	Magazine Reading : Effects					
		Good	%	Bad	%	Both	%
Below 25	40	15	37.5	10	25.0	15	37.5
26–35	60	20	33.3	8	13.3	32	53.3
36–45	.70	15	21.4	10	14.2	45	64.2
46 and above	30	7	23.3	3	10.0	20	66.6
Total	200	57	28.5	31	15.5	112	56.0

It is evident from the table 2.16 that 37.5 percent of the viewers hold the view that the effects of magazine reading are good whereas 25 percent of the viewers hold the view that the effects of magazine reading are bad and 37 percent of the viewers hold the view that the effects of magazine reading are both good and bad in the age group of below 25 years. 33.3 percent of the viewers hold the view that the effects of magazine reading are good whereas 13.3 percent of the viewers hold the view that the effects of magazine reading are bad and a majority of 53.3 percent of the viewers hold the view that the effects of magazine reading are both good and bad in the age group category of 26–35 years. 21.4 percent of the viewers hold the view that the effects of magazine reading are good whereas 14.2 percent of the viewers hold the view that the effects of magazine reading are bad and a majority of 64.2 percent of the viewers hold the view that the effects of magazine reading are both good and bad in the age group category of 36–45 years. 23.3 percent of the viewers hold the view that the effects of magazine reading are good whereas 10 percent of the viewers hold the view that the effects of magazine reading are bad and a majority 66.6 percent of the viewers hold the view that the effects of magazine reading are both good and bad in the age group category of 46 and above years.

It is also evident from the table that 28.5 percent of the total viewers hold the view that the effects of magazine reading are good whereas 15.5 percent of the total viewers hold the view that the effects of magazine reading are bad and a majority of 56 percent of the total viewers hold the view that the effects of magazine reading are both good and bad.

Table – 2.17

Knowledge of Computer/Internet

Age groups	N	Computer/Internet Knowing			
		Yes	%	No	%
Below 25	40	7	17.5	33	82.5
26–35	60	8	13.3	52	86.6

36–45	70	3	4.2	67	95.7
46 and above	30	1	3.3	29	96.6
Total	200	19	9.5	181	90.5

Regarding Knowledge of Computer/Internet, 17.5 percent of the viewers are knowing it whereas 82.5 percent of the viewers are not knowing computer/internet driving in the age group of below 25 years. 13.3 percent of the viewers are knowning computer/internet driving whereas 86.6 percent of the viewers are not knowing computer/internet driving in the age group of 26–35 years. Only 4.2 percent of the viewers are knowing computer/internet driving whereas 95.7 percent of the viewers are not knowing computer/internet driving in the age group of 36–45 years. Only 3.3 percent of the viewers are knowing computer/internet driving whereas 96.6 percent of the viewers are not knowing computer/internet driving in the age group of 46 and above years.

It is also evident from the table that only 9.5 percent of the total viewers are knowing computer/internet driving whereas a majority of 90.5 percent of the total viewers are not knowing computer/internet driving.

6

Doordarshan : Change and Development

For the analysis of change and development in relation to Doordarshan, a number of questions were asked about educational, social, cultural, occupational, political change, consciousness and development from the viewers are presented in classified and tabulated form for an interpretative and systematic analysis.

1. Educational Development

Table – 3.1
Education : Institution

Age group	N	Govt. Institution		Non-Govt. Institution	
		No.	%	No.	%
Below 25	35	15	42.8	20	57.1
26–35	55	25	45.4	30	54.5
36–45	60	35	58.3	25	41.6
46 and above	20	12	60.0	8	40.0
Total	170	87	51.1	83	48.8

It is evident from the table 3.1 that 42.8 percent of the viewers are educated from the institutions managed by government whereas 57.1 percent of the viewers are educated from the institutions managed by non-government agancies or by different missions in the age group category of below 25 years. 45.4 percent of the viewers are educated from those institutions which is managed by government whereas 54.5 percent of the viewers are educated from those institutions which is managed by non-government agencies or by different agencies in the age group category of 26-35 years. 58.3 percent of the viewers are educated from governmental institutions whereas 41.6 percent of the viewers are educated from non-governmental institutions in the age group of 36–45 years. 60 percent of the viewers are educated from the governmental institutions whereas 40 percent of the viewers are educated from the non-governmental institutions in the age group category of 46 and above years.

It is also evident from the table that 51.1 percent of the total viewers are educated from those institutions which is managed or controlled by the government whereas 48.8 percent of the total viewers are educated from those institutions which is managed or controlled by the non-government agencies or by the different missions. It is important to note here that there are so many educational institutions which is managed by Churches and other missions.

It is also important to note here that only 170 out of 200 viewers (85%) are educated whereas 30 out of 200 viewers (15%) are illiterate and they are not included in this table. Therefore, the total N is 170 = 100%

Table – 3.2

Co-education

Age group	N	Yes	%	No	%
Below 25	35	30	85.7	5	14.2

26–35	55	40	72.7	15	27.2
36–45	60	48	80.0	12	20.0
46 and above	20	12	60.0	8	40.0
Total	170	130	76.4	40	23.5

In the next question the viewers were asked 'is/was there co-education in your institution? The responses obtained from them are presented in table 3.2. It is evident from the table that 85.7 percent of the viewers replied in positive whereas 14.2 percent of the viewers replied in negative in the age group category below 25 years.72.7 percent of the viewers replied in positive whereas 27.2 percent of the viewers replied in negative in the age group category of 26–35 years. 80 percent of the viewers replied in positive whereas 20 percent of the viewers replied in negative in the age group category of 36–45 years. 60 percent of the viewers replied in positive whereas 40 percent of the viewers replied in negative in the age group category of 46 and above years.

It is also evident from the table that 76.4 percent of the total viewers replied in positive whereas 23.5 percent of the total viewers replied in negative.

Table – 3.3

Co-education : Needed

Age group	N	Yes	%	No	%
Below 25	5	5	100.0	–	–
26–35	15	15	100.0	–	–
36–45	12	11	91.6	1	8.3
46 and above	8	4	50.0	4	50.0
Total	40	35	87.5	5	12.5

The next question put to the viewers were 'if no, is it needed? The responses obtained from them are presented in table 3.3. It is evident from the table that 100 percent of the viewers replied that it is needed whereas not even a single viewer replied that it is not needed in the age group of below 25 years. 100 percent of the viewers replied that it is needed whereas not a single viewer replied that it is not needed in the age group category 26–35 years. 91.6 percent of the viewers replied that the co-education is needed whereas 8.3 percent of the viewers replied that it is not needed in the age group category of 36–45 years. 50 percent of the viewers replied that the co-education is needed whereas 50 percent of the viewers replied that it is not needed in the age group category of 46 and above years.

It is also evident from the table that 87.5 percent of the total viewers replied that co-education is needed whereas 12.5 percent of the viewers replied that co-education is not needed.

It is important to note here that only 40 (23.5%) out of total 170 (85 %) viewers are included in this table. Therefore, the total N is 40 = 100 %

Table – 3.4

Syllabus

Age group	N	Satisfied			
		Yes	%	No	%
Below 25	35	20	57.1	15	42.8
26–35	55	30	54.5	25	45.4
36–45	60	35	58.3	25	41.6
46 and above	20	15	75.0	5	25.0
Total	170	100	58.8	70	41.1

The question were asked to the viewers that 'Are/were you satisfied with your syllabus? The response obtained from them are presented in table 3.4. It is evident from the table that 57.1 percent of the viewers replied that they are/were satisfied with their syllabus whereas 42.8 percent of the viewers replied that they are/were not satisfied with their syllabus in the age group category of below 25 years. 54.5 percent of the viewers replied that they are/were satisfied with their syllabus whereas 45.4 percent of the viewers replied that they are/were not satisfied with their syllabus in the age group category of 26–35 years. 58.3 percent of the viewers replied that they are/were satisfied with their syllabus whereas 41.6 percent of the viewers replied that they are/were not satisfied with their syllabus in the age group category of 36–45 years. 75 percent of the viewers replied that they are/were satisfied with their syllabus whereas 25 percent of the viewers replied that they are/were not satisfied with their syllabus in the age group category of 46 and above years.

It is also evident from the table that 58.8 percent of the total viewers replied that they are/were satisfied with their syllabus whereas 41.1 percent of the viewers replied that they are/were not satisfied with their syllabus. The viewers hold the view that there should be a syllabus accordingly to the changing situation of the society.

It is important to note here that only 170 viewers (85%) out of 200 viewer (100%) are included in this table. 30 viewers (15%) out of 200 viewers are not included in this table because they are illiterate.

Table – 3.5

Campus Culture

Age groups	N	Good		Bad		Both	
		N	%	N	%	N	%
Below 25	40	20	50.0	10	25.0	10	25.0

26–35	60	20	33.3	15	25.0	25	41.6
36–45	70	15	21.4	15	21.4	40	57.1
46 and above	30	8	26.6	10	33.3	12	40.0
Total	200	63	31.5	50	25.0	87	43.5

The question put to the viewers were 'What is your opinion about campus culture'? The responses obtained from them are presented in table 3.5. It is evident from the table that 50 percent of the viewers hold the view that the campus culture is good whereas 25 percent of the viewers hold the view that the culture of the campus is bad and 25 percent of the viewers hold the view that the culture of the campus is both good and bad in the age group category of below 25 years. 33.3 percent of the viewers hold the view that the campus culture is good whereas 25 percent of the viewers hold the view that the campus culture is bad and 41.6 percent of the viewers hold the view that the culture of the campus is both good and bad in the age group category of 26–35 years. 21.4 percent of the viewers hold the view that the culture of the campus is good whereas 21.4 percent of the viewers hold the view that the culture campus is bad and 57.1 percent of the viewers hold the view that the culture of the campus is both good and bad in the age group category of 36–45 years. 26.6 percent of the viewers hold the view that the culture of the campus is good whereas 33.3 percent of the viewers hold the view that the culture of the campus is bad and 40 percent of the viewers hold the view that the campus culture is both good and bad in the age group category of 46 and above years.

It is also evident from the table that 31.5 percent of the total viewers hold the view that the culture of the campus is good whereas 25 percent of the total viewers hold the view that the campus culture is bad and 43.5 percent of the total viewers hold the view that the culture of the campus is both good and bad.

Table – 3.6

Sports

Age groups	N	Interested in Sports			
		Yes	%	No	%
Below 25	40	35	87.5	5	12.5
26–35	60	45	75.0	15	25.0
36–45	70	50	71.4	20	28.5
46 and above	30	20	66.6	10	33.3
Total	200	150	75.0	50	25.0

The question put to the viewers were 'Are you interested in sports'? The responses obtained from them are presented in table 3.6. It is evident from the table that 87.5 percent of the viewers are interested in sports whereas 12.5 percent of the viewers are not interested in sports in the age group category of below 25 years. 75 percent of the viewers are interested in sports whereas 25 percent of the viewers are not interested in sports in the age group category of 26–35 years. 71.4 percent of the viewers are not interested in sports whereas 28.5 percent of the viewers are not interested in sports in the age group category of 36–45 years. 66.6 percent of the viewers are interested in sports whereas 33.3 percent of the viewers are not interested in sports in the age group category of 46 and above years.

It is also evident from the table that 75 percent of the total viewers are interested in sports whereas 25 percent of the viewers are not interested in sports.

Table – 3.7

Extra-Curricular Activities

Age groups	N	Extra-Curricular Activities			
		Yes	%	No	%
Below 25	40	30	75.0	10	25.0
26–35	60	40	66.6	20	33.3
36–45	70	45	64.2	25	35.7
46 and above	30	20	66.6	10	33.3
Total	200	135	67.5	65	32.5

The question were asked to the viewers that 'Are you interested in extra-curricular activities'? The responses obtained from them are presented in table 3.7. It is evident from the table that 75 percent of the viewers are interested in extra-curricular activities whereas 25 percent of the viewers are not interested in extra-curricular activities in the age group category of below 25 years. 66.6 percent of the viewers are interested in extra-curricular activities whereas 33.3 percent of the viewers are not interested in extra-curricular activities in the age group of 26–35 years. 64.2 percent of the viewers are interested in extra-curricular activities whereas 35.7 percent of the viewers are not interested in extra-curricular activities in the age group category of 36-45 years. 66.6 percent of the viewers are interested in extra-curricular activities whereas 33.3 percent of the viewers are not interested in extra-curricular activities in the age group category of 46 and above years.

It is also evident from the table that 67.5 percent of the total viewers are interested in extra curricular activities whereas 32.5 percent of the viewers are not interested in extra-curricular activities.

It is important to note here that the people of Jharkhand specially tribal like sports very much, games such as Hockey, Kabbaddi etc. Hunting, singing, dance and music are the life of tribal people.

Table – 3.8

Education and Children

Age groups	N	Education of Children			
		Yes	%	No	%
Below 25	40	40	100.0	–	–
26–35	60	60	100.0	–	–
36–45	70	65	92.8	5	7.1
46 and above	30	23	76.6	7	23.3
Total	200	188	94.0	12	6.0

The next question put to the viewers were 'Are you interested to educate your children'? The responses obtained from them are presented in table 3.8. It is evident from table that 100 percent of the viewers are interested to educate their children and not a single viewer replied in negative in the age group of below 25 years. It is evident that 100 percent of the viewers in the age group of 26–35 years are interested to educate their children and not a single viewer replied in negative. 92.8 percent of the viewers are interested to educated their children whereas only 7.1 percent of the viewers are not interested to educate their children because of economic crisis in the age group of 36–45 years. 76.6 percent of the viewers are interested to educate their children whereas 23.3 percent of the viewers are not interested to educated their children because of the same reason in the age group of 46 and above years.

It is also evident from the table that 94 percent of the total viewers are interested to educate their children whereas only 6 percent of the total viewers are not interested to educate their children.

Table – 3.9

Medium of Education

Age group	N	Medium					
		Mother Tongue		Hindi		English	
		N	%	N	%	N	%
Below 25	40	12	30.0	3	7.5	25	62.5
26–35	60	16	26.6	4	6.6	40	66.6
36–45	65	23	35.3	2	3.0	40	61.5
46 and above	23	10	43.4	2	8.6	11	47.8
Total	188	61	32.4	11	5.8	116	61.7

The next question were asked to the viewers that 'What will be the medium of education of your children'? The responses obtained from them are presented in table 3.9. It is evident from the table that 30 percent of the viewers hold the view that the medium of education of their children will be the mother tongue whereas 7.5 percent of the viewers hold the view that the medium of education of their children will be Hindi language and a majority of 62.5 percent of the viewers hold the view that the medium of education of their children will be English language in the age group of below 25 years. 26.6 percent of the viewers hold the view that the medium of education of their children will be mother tongue whereas 6.6 percent of the viewers hold the view that the medium of education of their children will be Hindi and a majority of 66.6 percent of the viewers hold the view that the medium of education of their children will be English in the age group of 26–35 years. 35.3 percent of the viewers hold the view that the medium of education of their children will be mother tongue whereas only 3 percent of the viewers hold the view that the medium of education of their children will be Hindi and a majority of 61.5 percent of the viewers hold the view that the medium of education of their children will be English in the age group of 36–45 years. 43.4 percent of the viewers hold the view that the medium of education of their children will be mother tongue whereas 8.6 percent of the viewers hold the view that the medium of education of their children will be Hindi and a majority of 47.8 percent of the viewers hold the view that the medium of education of their children will be English in the age group of 46 and above years.

It is also evident from the table that 32.4 percent of the total viewers hold the view that the medium of education of their children will be mother tongue whereas only 5.8 percent of the total viewers hold the view that the medium of education of their children will be Hindi and a majority of 61.7 percent of the total viewers hold the view that the medium of education of their children will be English language.

It is important to note here that 188 (94%) out of 200 viewers are included in this table. 6 percent of the viewers are not interested to educate their children, therefore they are not included in this table. Hence the total n is 188 = 100%.

Table – 3.10

Impact of Doordarshan on Education

Age group	N	Impact			
		Yes	%	No	%
Below 25	40	40	100.0	–	–

26–35	60	60	100.0	–	–
36-45	70	70	100.0	–	–
46 and above	30	30	100.0	–	–
Total	200	200	100.0	–	–

The question put to the viewers were 'Is there impact of Doordarshan on education'? The responses obtained from them are presented in table 3.10. It is evident from the table that 100 percent of the viewers in different age groups hold the view that there is a lot of impact of Doordarshan on education and educational activities. They replied that there are so many programmes related to educational activities, personality development and general awareness. These programmes are directly related to an individual, the family, society and nation.

(II) Social Consciousness and Development

Question pertaining to the above were asked from the viewers in relation to the impact of Doordarshan. These are presented in classified and tabulated form for an interpretative and systematic analysis.

Table – 4.1

Should women have equal right as men?

Age groups	N	Should women have equal right as men?			
		Yes	%	No	%
Below 25	40	35	87.5	4	12.5
26–35	60	45	75.0	15	25.0
36–45	70	50	71.4	20	28.5
46 and above	30	20	66.6	10	33.3
Total	200	150	75.0	50	25.0

The question were asked to the viewers that 'Should women have equal right as men in the society'? the responses obtained from them are presented in table 4.1. It is evident from the table that 87.5 percent of the viewers hold the view that women should have equal right as men in the society where are 12.5 percent of the viewers hold the view that women should not have equal right as men in the society in the age group of below 25 years. 75 percent of the viewers hold the view that women should have equal right as men whereas 25 percent of the viewers hold the view that women should not have equal right as men in the society in the age group of 26–35 years. 71.4 percent of the viewers hold the view that women should have equal right as men in the society whereas 28.5 percent of the viewers hold the view that women should not have equal right as men in the society in the age group of 36–45 years and 66.6 percent of the viewers hold the view that women should have equal right as men whereas 33.3 percent of the viewers hold the view that women should not have equal right as men in the society in the age group of 46 and above.

It is also evident from the table that 75 percent of the total viewers hold the view that women should have equal right as men whereas 25 percent of the total viewers hold the view that women should not have equal right as men in the society.

It is important to note that only 50 viewers (25%) out of 200 viewers hold the view that women should not have equal right as men in the society. In the tribal society the status of women is very high and the women are much laborious in comparison to men. Women are earning money and doing house-hold work very nicely. But they are still exploited by the exploiters. In the marriage system 'Bride price' is very common.

Table – 4.2

Family Planning Programme

Age groups	N	Family Planning Programme : Right			
		Yes	%	No	%
Below 25	40	38	95.0	2	5.0
26–35	60	45	75.0	15	25.0
36–45	70	50	71.4	20	28.5
46 and above	30	20	66.6	10	33.3
Total	200	153	76.5	47	23.5

The next question asked to the viewers were 'Do you think that family planning programme is right'? The responses obtained from them are presented in table 4.2. It is evident from the table that 95 percent of the viewers hold the view that family planning programme is right whereas only 5 percent of the viewers hold the view that family planning programme is wrong in the age group category of below 25 years. 75 percent of the viewers hold the view that the family planning programme is right whereas 25 percent of the viewers hold the view that family planning programme is wrong in the age group category of 26–35 years. 71.4 percent of the viewers hold the view that family planning programme is right whereas 28.5 percent of the viewers hold the view that family programme is wrong in the age group category of 36–45 years. 66.6 percent of the viewers hold the view that family planning programme is right whereas 33.3 percent of the viewers hold the view family planning programme is wrong in the age group category of 46 and above years.

It is also evident from the table that 76.5 percent of the total viewers hold the view that family planning programme is right whereas 23.5 percent of the viewers hold the view that family planning programme is wrong.

Table – 4.3
Women's Liberation

Age groups	N	Women's Liberation : Right			
		Yes	%	No	%
Below 25	40	35	87.5	5	12.5
26–35	60	40	66.6	20	33.3
36–45	70	40	57.1	30	42.8
46 and above	30	20	66.6	10	33.3
Total	200	135	67.5	65	32.5

The next question that was put forth to the viewers 'do you think that women's liberation is right'? The responses obtained from them are presented in table 4.3. It is evident from the table that 87.5 percent of the viewers hold the view that the women's liberation is right whereas 12.5 percent of the viewers hold the view that women's liberation is wrong in the age group category of below 25 years. 66.6 percent of the viewers hold the view that women's liberation is right whereas 33.3 percent of the viewers hold the view that women's liberation is wrong in the age group category of 26–35 years. 57.1 percent of the viewers hold the view that women's liberation is right whereas 42.8 percent of the viewers hold the view that women's liberation is wrong in the age group category of 36–45 years. 66.6 percent of the viewers hold the view that women's liberation is right whereas 33.3 percent of the viewers hold the view that women's liberation is wrong in the age group category of 46 and above years.

It is also evident from the table that 67.5 percent of the total viewers hold the view that women's liberation is right whereas 32.5 percent of the viewers hold the view that women's liberation is wrong.

Table – 4.4

Inter-Caste Marriage

Age group	N	Inter-caste Marriage			
		Yes	%	No	%
Below 25	40	38	95.0	2	5.0
26–35	60	40	66.6	20	33.3
36–45	70	40	57.1	30	42.8
46 and above	30	20	66.6	10	33.3
Total	200	138	69.0	62	31.0

The viewers were asked that whether 'Inter-caste marriages should be encouraged'? The responses obtained from them are presented in table 4.4. It is evident from the table that 95 percent of the viewers hold the view that inter-caste marriages should be encouraged whereas only 5 percent of the viewers hold the view that inter-caste marriages should not be encouraged in the age group category of below 25 years. 66.6 percent of the viewers hold the view that inter-caste marriages should be encouraged whereas 33.3 percent of the viewers hold the view that inter-caste marriages should not be encouraged in the age group of 26–35 years. 57.1 percent of the viewers hold the view that inter-caste marriages should be encouraged whereas 42.8 percent of the viewers hold the view that inter-caste marriages should not be encouraged in the age group category of 36–45 years. 66.6 percent of the viewers hold the view that inter-caste marriages should be encouraged whereas 33.3 percent of the viewers hold the view that inter-caste marriages should not be encouraged in the age group category of 46 and above years.

It is also evident from the table that 69 percent of the total viewers hold the view that inter-caste marriages should be encouraged whereas 31 percent of the total viewers hold the view that inter-caste marriages should not be encouraged.

It is important to note that there are so many viewers hold the view that inter-tribal marriages should also be encouraged. They accepts that inter-tribal marriages are still very limited in the society.

Table – 4.5

Changing Marriage System

Age groups	N	Changing marriage system			
		Yes	%	No	%
Below 25	40	35	87.5	5	12.5
26–35	60	50	83.3	10	16.6
36–45	70	60	85.7	10	14.2
46 and above	30	25	83.3	5	16.6
Total	200	170	85.0	30	15.0

The question were asked to the viewers that 'Do you think that the marriage system is changing? The responses obtained from them are presented in table 4.5. It is evident from the table that 87.5 percent of the viewers hold the view that marriage system is changing whereas 12.5 percent of the viewers hold the view that marriage system is not changing in the age group category of below 25 years. 83.3 percent of the viewers hold the view that marriage system is changing whereas 16.6 percent of the viewers hold the view that marriage system is not changing in the age group of 26–35 years. 85.7 percent of the viewers hold the view that marriage system is changing whereas 14.2 percent of the viewers hold the view that marriage system is not changing.(36–45 age group) 83.3 percent of the viewers hold the view that marriage system is changing whereas 16.6 percent of the viewers hold the view that marriage system is not changing.(46 and above)

It is also evident from the table that 85 percent of the total viewers hold the view that marriage system is changing whereas 15 percent of the viewers hold the view that marriage system is not changing.

Table – 4.6

Family Structure

Age groups	N	Changing Family Structure			
		Yes	%	No	%
Below 25	40	39	97.5	1	2.5
26–35	60	57	95.0	3	5.0
36–45	70	65	92.8	5	7.1
46 and above	30	28	93.3	2	6.6
Total	200	189	94.5	11	5.5

Viewers were asked that 'Do they think that family structure is changing'? The responses obtained from them are presented in table 4.6. It is evident from the table that 97.5 percent of the viewers hold the view that the family structure is changing whereas 2.5 percent of the viewers hold the view that family structure is not changing in the age group of below 25 years. 95 percent of the viewers hold the view that the family structure is changing whereas 5 percent of the viewers hold the view that the family structure is not changing in the age group category of 26–35 years. 92.8 percent of the viewers hold the view that the family structure is changing whereas 7.1 percent of the viewers hold the view that the family structure is not changing in the age group category of 36–45 years. 93.3 percent of the viewers hold the view that the family structure is changing whereas 6.6 percent of the viewers hold the view that the family structure is not changing in the age group category of 46 and above years.

The table shows that 94.5 percent of the total viewers hold the view that the family structure is changing whereas 5.5 percent of the total viewers hold the view that the family structure is not changing.

Table – 4.7

Doordarshan and Social Consciousness

Age groups	N	Impact of Doordarshan			
		Yes	%	No	%
Below 25	40	40	100.0	–	–
26–35	60	60	100.0	–	–
36–45	70	70	100.0	–	–
46 and above	30	30	100.0	–	–
Total	200	200	100.0	–	–

The question were asked to the viewers that 'Do you think that there is impact of Doordarshan on social consciousness and development'? The responses obtained from them are presented in table 4.7. It is evident from the table that 100 percent of the viewers in each of the age group hold the view that there is impact of Doordarshan on social consciousness and development of an individual or the society.

(III) Economic and Occupational Development

Questions that were asked from the viewers about their economic and occupational change and development in relation to the impact of Doordarshan have been presented in classified and tabulated form for an interpretative and systematic analysis.

Table – 5.1

Occupation/Job : Satisfaction

Age groups	N	Occupation/Job : Satisfation			
		Yes	%	No	%
Below 25	10	4	40.0	6	60.0
26–35	50	30	60.0	20	40.0
36–45	50	35	70.0	15	30.0
46 and above	20	15	75.0	5	25.0
Total	130	84	64.6	46	35.3

The question put to the viewers were 'Are you satisfied with your occupation/job'? The responses obtained from them are presented in table 5.1. It is evident from the table that 40 percent of the viewers are satisfied with their occupation/job whereas 60 percent of the viewers are not satisfied with the occupation/job in the age group of below 25 years. 60 percent of the viewers are satisfied with their occupation/job whereas 40 percent of the viewers are not satisfied with their occupation/job in the age group category of 26–35 years. 70 percent of the viewers are satisfied with their occupation/job whereas 30 percent of the viewers are not satisfied with their occupation/job in the age group of 36–45 years. 75 percent of the viewers are satisfied with their occupation/job whereas 25 percent of the viewers are not satisfied with their occupation/job in the age group category of 46 and above years.

It is also evident from the table that 64.6 percent of the viewers are satisfied with their occupation/job whereas 35.3 percent of the viewers are not satisfied with their occupation/job.

It is important to note that only 130 (65%) out of 200 viewers are included in this table. 70 (35%) out of 200 viewers are not included in this table because they are not working in terms of money earning. Hence, the total N is 130 = 100%.

Table – 5.2

Occupation/Job : Change

Age groups	N	Change in Occupation/Job			
		Yes	%	No	%
Below 25	10	6	60.0	4	40.0
26–35	50	40	80.0	10	20.0
36–45	50	20	40.0	30	60.0
46 and above	20	10	50.0	10	50.0
Total	130	76	58.4	54	41.5

The next question asked to the viewers that 'Would you like to change your occupation/job in near future'? The responses obtained from them are presented in table 5.2. It is evident from the table that 60 percent of the viewers hold the view that they like to change their occupation/job in near future whereas 40 percent of the viewers replied in negative in the age group category of below 25 years. 80 percent of the viewers hold the view that they like to change their occupation/job in near future whereas 20 percent of the viewers replied in negative in the age group category of 26–35 years. 40 percent of the viewers hold the view that they like to change their occupation/job in near future whereas 60 percent of the viewers replied in negative in the age group category of 36–45 years. 50 percent of the viewers hold the view that they like to change their occupation/job in near future whereas 50 percent of the viewers replied in negative in the age group category of 46 and above years.

This table shows that 58.4 percent of the total viewers hold the view that they like to change their occupation/job in near future whereas 41.5 percent of the total viewers replied in negative.

It is important to note that only 130 (65%) out of 200 viewers are included in this table because they are earning in terms of money.

Table – 5.3

Mobility

Age group	N	Mobility			
		Yes	%	No	%
Below 25	40	30	75.0	10	25.0
26–35	60	40	66.6	20	33.3
36–45	70	30	42.8	40	57.1
46 and above	30	5	16.6	25	83.3
Total	200	105	52.5	95	47.5

Viewers were asked that 'Would you like to go to other places for better working conditions'? The responses obtained from them are presented in table 5.3. It is evident from the table that 75 percent of the viewers like to go to other places for better working conditions whereas 25 percent of the viewers replied in negative in the age group category of below 25 years. 66.6 percent of the viewers like to go to other places for better working conditions whereas 33.3 percent of the viewers replied in negative in the age group category of 26–35 years. 42.8 percent of the viewers like to go to other places for better working conditions whereas 57.1 percent of the viewers replied in negative in the age group category of 36–45 years. 16.6 percent of the viewers like to go to other places for better working conditions whereas 83.3 percent of the viewers replied in negative in the age group of 46 and above years.

The table further shows that 52.5 percent of the total viewers like to go to other places for better working conditions whereas 47.5 percent of the viewers replied in negative.

Table – 5.4

Savings

Age groups	N	Savings			
		Yes	%	No	%
Below 25	40	20	50.0	20	50.0
26–35	60	35	58.3	25	41.6
36–45	70	35	50.0	35	50.0
46 and above	30	20	66.6	10	33.3
Total	200	110	55.0	90	45.0

Viewers were asked that 'Do they like to save'? The responses obtained from them are presented in table 5.4. The table shows that 50 percent of the viewers like to save whereas 50 percent of the viewers replied in negative in the age group category of below 25 years. 58.3 percent of the viewers like to save whereas 41.6 percent of the viewers replied in negative in the age group category of 26–35 years. 50 percent of the viewers like to save whereas 50 percent of the viewers replied in negative in the age group category of 36–45 years. 66.6 percent of the viewers like to save whereas 33.3

percent of the viewers replied in negative in the age group category of 46 and above years

It is evident from the table that 55 percent of the viewers like to save whereas 45 percent of the viewers replied in negative.

Table – 5.5

Standard of Living

Age groups	N	Satisfied			
		Yes	%	No	%
Below 25	40	10	25.0	30	75.0
26–35	60	20	33.3	40	66.6
36–45	70	25	35.7	45	64.2
46 and above	30	10	33.3	20	66.6
Total	200	65	32.5	135	67.5

The next question asked to the viewers was that 'Are they satisfied with their standard of living'? The responses obtained from them are presented in table 5.5. It is evident from the table that 25 percent of the viewers are satisfied with their standard of living whereas 75 percent of the viewers are not satisfied with their standard of living in the age group category of below 25 years. 33.3 percent of the viewers are satisfied with their standard of living whereas 66.6 percent of the viewers are not satisfied with their standard of living in the age group category of 26–35 years. 35.7 percent of the viewers are satisfied with their standard of living whereas 64.2 percent of the viewers are not satisfied with their standard of living in the age group category of 36–45 years. 33.3 percent of the viewers are satisfied with their standard of living where 66.6 percent of the viewers are not satisfied with their standard of living in the age group category of 46 and above years.

The table further shows that 32.5 percent of the total viewers are satisfied with their standard of living whereas 67.5 percent of the total viewers are not satisfied with the standard of living.

It means that a majority of viewers are not satisfied with their standard of living but they are optimistic and think that their standard of living will be better after formation of the Jharkhand as state.

Table – 5.6

Govt. Economic Programmes

Age group	N	Economic Programmes			
		Yes	%	No	%
Below 25	40	35	87.5	5	12.5
26–35	60	45	75.0	15	25.0
36–45	70	40	57.1	30	42.8
46 and above	30	18	60.0	12	40.0
Total	200	138	69.0	62	31.0

The question asked to the viewers was that 'Do you know about the economic programmes of the government'? The responses obtained from them are presented in table 5.6. The table shows that 87.5 percent of the viewers know the economic programmes of the government whereas 12.5 percent of the viewers replied in negative in the age group category of below 25 years. 75 percent of the viewers know the economic programmes of the government whereas 25 percent of the viewers replied in negative in the age group category of 26–35 years. 57.1 percent of the viewers know the economic programmes of government whereas

42.8 percent of the viewers replied in negative in the age group category of 36–45 years. 60 percent of the viewers know the economic programmes of government whereas 40 percent of the viewers replied in negative in the age group category of 46 and above years.

The table further shows that 69 percent of the total viewers know the economic programmes of government whereas 31 percent of the total viewers replied in negative.

Table – 5.7

Doordarshan and Economic Development

Age group	N	Impact of Doordarshan on Economic Development			
		Yes	%	No	%
Below 25	40	40	100.0	–	–
26–35	60	60	100.0	–	–
36–45	70	70	100.0	–	–
46 and above	30	30	100.0	–	–
Total	200	200	100.0	–	–

Viewers was asked that 'Is there any impact of Doordarshan on economic and occupational change'? The responses obtained from them are presented in table 5.7. It is evident from the table that 100 percent of the viewers in each age group hold the view that there is impact of Doordarshan on economic and occupational change.

(IV) Cultural Development

A number of questions were asked from the viewers about their cultural development. These are presented in classified and tabulated form for an interpretative and systematic analysis.

Table – 6.1

Festivals

Age groups	N	Participation in Festivals			
		Yes	%	No	%
Below 25	40	40	100.0	–	–
26–35	60	58	96.6	2	3.3
36–45	70	65	92.8	5	7.1
46 and above	30	25	83.3	5	16.6
Total	200	188	94.0	12	6.0

In reply to the question posed to the viewers that 'Did you participated in festival'? Their responses are presented with the help of table 6.1. The table shows that 100 percent of the viewers have participated in festivals in the age group category of below 25 years. 96.6 percent of the viewers has participated in festivals whereas only 3.3 percent of the viewers have not participated in festivals in the age group category of 26–35 years. 92.8 percent of the viewers have participated in festivals whereas only 7.1 percent of the viewers have not participated in festivals in the age group category of 36–45 years. 83.3 percent of the viewers have participated in festivals whereas only 16.6 percent of the viewers has not participated in festivals in the age group of 46 and above years.

The table further shows that 94 percent of the total viewers has participated in festivals whereas only 6 percent of the viewers have not participated in festivals.

Table – 6.2

Dress

Age groups	N	Changing Dress Pattern : Liking			
		Yes	%	No	%
Below 25	40	35	87.5	5	12.5
26–35	60	45	75.0	15	25.0
36–45	70	50	71.4	20	28.5
46 and above	30	20	66.6	10	33.3
Total	200	150	75.0	50	25.0

The next question asked to the viewers was that 'Do they like the changes in dress pattern'? The responses obtained from them are presented in table 6.2. The table shows that 87.5 percent of the viewers like the changes in dress pattern whereas only 12.5 percent of the viewers replied in negative in the age group category of below 25 years. 75 percent of the viewers like the changes in dress pattern whereas only 25 percent of the viewers are not liking the changes in dress pattern in the age group category of 26–35 years. 71.4 percent of the viewers are liking the changes in dress pattern whereas only 28.5 percent of the viewers are not liking the changes in dress pattern in the age group category of 36–45 years. 66.6 percent of the viewers are liking the changes in dress pattern whereas only 33.3 percent of the viewers are not liking the changes in dress pattern in the age group category of 46 and above years.

It is evident from the table that 75 percent of the total viewers are liking the changes in dress pattern whereas only 25 percent of the viewers are not liking the changes in dress pattern.

Table – 6.3

Music and Instruments

Age groups	N	Interested in Music and Instruments			
		Yes	%	No	%
Below 25	40	40	100.0	–	–
26–35	60	58	96.6	2	3.3
36–45	70	65	92.8	5	7.1
46 and above	30	25	83.3	5	16.6
Total	200	188	94.0	12	6.0

The question were asked to the viewers that 'Are you interested in music and instruments'? The responses obtained from them are presented in table 6.3 the table shows that 100 percent of the viewers are interested in music and instruments in the age group category below 25 years. 96.6 percent of the viewers are interested in music and instruments whereas only 3.3 percent of the viewers are not interested in music and instruments in the age group category of 26–35 years. 92.8 percent of the viewers are interested in music and instruments whereas only. 7.1 percent of the viewers are not interested in music and instruments in the age group category of 36–45 years. 83.3 percent of the viewers are interested in music and instruments whereas only 16.6 percent of the viewers are not interested in music and instruments in the age group category of 46 and above years.

The table further shows that a majority of 94 percent of the viewers are interested in music and instruments whereas only 6 percent of the viewers are not interested in music and instruments.

Table – 6.4

Food Habits

Age groups	N	Changing Food Habits			
		Yes	%	No	%
Below 25	40	40	100.0	–	–
26–35	60	60	100.0	–	–
36–45	70	70	100.0	–	–
46 and above	30	30	100.0	–	–
Total	200	200	100.0	–	–

Viewers were asked that 'Do they like the changes in food habits'? The responses obtained from them are presented in table 6.4. It is evident from the table that 100 percent of the viewers in each age group category are liking the changes in their food habits.

Table – 6.5

Membership : Club/Other Organizations

Age groups	N	Membership			
		Yes	%	No	%
Below 25	40	25	62.5	15	37.5
26–35	60	40	66.6	20	33.3
36–45	70	30	42.8	40	57.1
46 and above	30	10	33.3	20	66.6
Total	200	105	52.5	95	47.5

The question were asked to the viewers that 'Are you a member of any club or any cultural organization? The responses obtained from them are presented in table 6.5. It is evident from the table that 62.5 percent of the viewers are the members of the clubs or other cultural organizations whereas 67.5 percent of the viewers are not the members of any clubs or any other organizations in the age group of below 25 years. 66.6 percent of the viewers are the members of the clubs or any other cultural organizations whereas 33.3 percent of the viewers are not the members of any clubs or any other cultural organizations in the age group of 26 to 35 years. 42.8 percent of the viewers are the members of the clubs or other cultural organization whereas 57.1 percent of the viewers are not the members of any clubs or any other cultural organizations in the age group of 36 to 45 years. 33.3 percent of the viewers are the members of the clubs or other cultural organizations whereas 66.6 percent of the viewers are not the members of any clubs or any other cultural organizations in the age group of 46 and above years.

It is also evident from the table that 52.5 percent of the total viewers are the members of the clubs or other cultural organizations whereas 47.5 percent of the total viewers are not the members of any clubs or any other cultural organizations.

It means that majority of the viewers are the members of the clubs or other cultural organizations.

Table – 6.6

Belief in Magic etc.

Age groups	N	Belief			
		Yes	%	No	%
Below 25	40	15	37.5	25	62.5
26–35	60	20	33.3	40	66.6
36–45	70	30	42.8	40	57.1
46 and above	30	20	66.6	10	33.3
Total	200	85	42.5	115	57.5

The question were asked to the viewers that 'Do you believe in magic etc'. The responses obtained from them are presented in table 6.6. It is evident from the table that 37.5 percent of the viewers believe in magic etc. whereas 62.5 percent of the viewers do not believe in these things in the age group category of below 25 years. 33.3 percent of the viewers believe in magic etc. whereas 66.6 percent of the viewers do not believe in magic etc. in the age group category of 26-35 years. 42.8 percent of the viewers believe in magic etc. whereas 57.1 percent of the viewers do not believe in these things in the age group category of 36–45 years. 66.6 percent of the viewers believe in magic etc. whereas 33.3 percent of the viewers do not believe in these things in the age group category of 46 and above years.

It is also evident from the table that 42.5 percent of the total viewers believe in magic etc. whereas 57.5 percent of the total viewers do not believe in magic and these things.

It means that majority of the viewers do not believe in magic and these things. Perhaps it is because of fast educational developments and scientific advancement and the impact of media awareness.

Table – 6.7

Doordarshan and Cultural Development

Age groups	N	Impact of Doordarshan on Cultural Development			
		Yes	%	No	%
Below 25	40	40	100.0	–	–
26–35	60	60	100.0	–	–
36–45	70	70	100.0	–	–
46 and above	30	30	100.0	–	–
Total	200	200	100.0	–	–

The question were asked to the viewers that 'Is there impact of Doordarshan on their culture'? The responses obtained from them are presented in table 6.7. The table shows that 100 percent of the viewers in each of the age group category hold the view that there is impact of Doordarshan on their culture.

(V) Political Development

A number of questions were asked to the viewers about their political development. The responses obtained from them are presented in tabulated form for the systematic analysis.

Table – 7.1

Political Party

Age groups	N	Relation to Political Party			
		Yes	%	No	%
Below 25	40	15	37.5	25	62.5
26–35	60	20	33.3	40	66.6
36–45	70	25	35.7	45	64.2
46 and above	30	5	16.6	25	83.3
Total	200	65	32.5	135	67.5

The question were asked to the viewers that 'Are they related to any political party'? The responses from them are presented in table 7.1. It is evident from the table that 37.5 percent of the viewers are related to different political parties whereas 62.5 percent of the viewers are not related to any political parties in the age group of below 25 years. 33.3 percent of the viewers are related to political parties whereas 66.6 percent of the viewer are not related to political parties in the age group of 26–35 years. 35.7 percent of the viewers are related to political parties whereas 64.2 percent of the viewers are not related to political parties in the age group of 36–45 years. 16.6 percent of the viewers are related to political parties whereas 83.3 percent of the viewers are not related to political parties in the age group of 46 and above years.

The table further shows that 32.5 percent of the total viewers are related to political parties whereas 67.5 percent of the viewers are not related to political parties.

Table – 7.2
Vote

Age group	N	Voting			
		Yes	%	No	%
Below 25	40	35	87.5	5	12.5
26–35	60	30	50.0	30	50.0
36–45	70	25	35.7	45	64.2
46 and above	30	10	33.3	20	66.6
Total	200	100	50.0	100	50.0

Viewers were asked that 'Did they cast their vote in the last election'? It is evident from the table 7.2 that 87.5 percent of the viewers did cast their vote in the last election whereas 12.5 percent of the viewers did not cast their vote in the last election in the age group category of below 25 years. 50 percent of the viewers did cast their vote in the last election whereas 50 percent of the viewers did not cast their vote in the last election in the age group category of 26–35 years. 35.7 percent of the viewers did cast their vote in the last election whereas 64.2 percent of the viewers did not cast their vote in the last election in the age group of 36–45 years. 33.3 percent of the viewer did cast their vote in the last election whereas 66.6 percent of the viewers did not cast their vote in the last election in the age group of 46 and above years.

The table further shows that 50 percent of the total viewers did cast their vote in the last election whereas 50 percent of the viewers did not cast their vote in the last election.

Table – 7.3

Participation of Women

Age groups	N	Participation of Women			
		Yes	%	No	%
Below 25	40	30	75.0	10	25.0
26–35	60	35	58.3	25	41.6
36–45	70	20	28.5	50	71.4
46 and above	30	7	23.3	23	76.6
Total	200	92	46.0	108	54.0

The question were asked to the viewers that whether 'Women participated in the last election'? The responses obtained from them are presented in table 7.3. It is evident from the table that 75 percent of the viewers hold the view that women did participate in the last election whereas 25 percent of the viewers hold the view that women did not participate in the last election in the age group category of below 25 years. 58.3 percent of the viewers hold the view that women did participate in the last election whereas 41.6 percent of the viewers hold the view that women did not participate in the last election in the age group category of 26–35 years. 28.5 percent of the viewers hold the view that women did participate in the last election whereas 71.4 percent of the viewers hold the view that women did not participate in the last election in the age group category of 36–45 years. 23.3 percent of the viewers hold the view that women did participate in the last election whereas 76.6 percent of the viewers hold the view that women did not participate in the last election in the age group category of 46 and above years.

It is also evident from the table that 46 percent of the total viewers hold the view that women did participate in the last election whereas 54 percent of the total viewers hold the view the women did not participate in the last election.

It means that majority of viewers hold the view that women did not participate in the last election.

The table shows that majority of women did not participate in the last election. Perhaps it is because the load of house–hold works and there is no time for these political awareness. It is also because, they are not actively associated with the political parties. Women are still suffering from lack of political awareness.

Table – 7.4

Reservation

Age groups	N	Reservation			
		Yes	%	No	%
Below 25	40	40	100.0	–	–
26–35	60	60	100.0	–	–
36–45	70	70	100.0	–	–
46 and above	30	30	100.0	–	–
Total	200	200	100.0	–	–

The next question that was asked to the viewers 'Is reservation necessary'? It is evident from the table 7.4 that 100 percent of the viewers in each category of age group hold the view that reservation is necessary.

Table – 7.5

Doordarshan and Political Development

Age groups	N	Impact of Doordarshan on Political Development			
		Yes	%	No	%
Below 25	40	40	100.0	–	–
26–35	60	60	100.0	–	–
36–45	70	70	100.0	–	–
46 and above	30	30	100.0	–	–
Total	200	200	100.0	–	–

The question were asked to the viewers that 'Is there impact of Doordarshan on political development'? The table 7.5 shows that 100 percent of the viewers in each category of age group hold the view that there is impact of Doordarshan on political activities.

(VI) Continuity and Change

A number of question were asked from the viewers about continuity and change. The responses are presented in tabulated form for the systematic analysis.

Table – 8.1

Belief in Religion

Age groups	N	Belief in religion			
		Yes	%	No	%
Below 25	40	40	100.0	–	–
26–35	60	60	100.0	–	–
36–45	70	70	100.0	–	–
46 and above	30	30	100.0	–	–
Total	200	200	100.0	–	–

Viewers were asked that 'Do they believe in religion'? It is evident from the table 8.1 that 100 percent of the viewers in each age group do believe in religion.

Table – 8.2

Old Values

Age groups	N	Old Values : Change			
		Yes	%	No	%
Below 25	40	35	87.5	5	12.5
26–35	60	45	75.0	15	25.0
36–45	70	50	71.4	20	28.5
46 and above	30	20	66.6	10	33.3
Total	200	150	75.0	50	25.0

The next question put forth to the viewers was that 'Are the old values changing'? The responses obtained from them are presented in table 8.2. It is evident from the table that 87.5 percent of the viewers hold the view that the old values are changing whereas 12.5 percent of the viewers hold the view that the old values are not changing in the age group of below 25 years. 75 percent of the viewers hold the view that the old values are changing whereas 25 percent of the viewers hold the view that the old values are not changing in the age group of 26–35 years. 71.4 percent of the viewers hold the view that the old values are changing whereas 28.5 percent of the viewers hold the view that the old values are not changing in the age group of 36–45 years. 66.6 percent of the viewers hold the view that the old values are changing whereas 33.3 percent of the viewers hold the view that the old values are not changing in the age group of 46 and above years.

The table further shows that 75 percent of the total viewers hold the view that the old values are changing whereas 25 percent of the viewers hold the view that the old values are not changing.

It means that a majority of viewers hold the view that the old values are changing and the new values are coming very fast in the society.

Table – 8.3

Traditional Ways

Age groups	N	Honor the Traditional Ways			
		Yes	%	No	%
Below 25	40	15	37.5	25	62.5
26–35	60	25	41.6	35	58.3
36–45	70	30	42.8	40	57.1
46 and above	30	20	66.6	10	33.3
Total	200	90	45.0	110	55.0

The question were asked to the viewers that 'Should we honor the traditional ways'? The responses obtained from them are presented in table 8.3. It is evident from the table that 37.5 percent of the viewers hold the view that we should honor the traditional ways whereas 62.5 percent of the viewers hold the view that we should not honor the traditional ways in the age group category of below 25 years. 41.6 percent of the viewers hold the view that we should honor the traditional ways whereas 58.3 percent of the viewers hold the view that we should not honor the traditional ways in the age group category of 26–35 years. 42.8 percent of the viewers hold the view that we should honor the traditional ways whereas 57.1 percent of the viewers hold the view that we should not honor the traditional ways in the age group category of 36–45 years. 66.6 percent of the viewers hold the view that we should honor the traditional ways whereas 33.3 percent of the viewers hold the view that we should not honor the traditional ways in the age group category of 46 and above years.

The table further shows that 45 percent of the total viewers hold the view that we should honour the traditional ways whereas 55 percent of the total viewers hold the view that we should not honour the traditional ways.

It means that most of the viewers hold the view that they are honouring the traditional ways.

Table – 8.4
Inter-Caste Dining

Age groups	N	Inter-caste dining			
		Yes	%	No	%
Below 25	40	35	87.5	5	12.5
26–35	60	45	75.0	15	25.0
36–45	70	25	35.7	45	64.2
46 and above	30	10	33.3	20	66.6
Total	200	115	57.5	85	42.5

Viewers were asked that 'Is there be Inter-caste dining in the society'? The responses obtained from them are presented in table 8.4. It is evident from the table that 87.5 percent of the viewers hold the view that there should be inter-caste dining in the society whereas 12.5 percent of the viewers hold the view that there should not be inter-caste dining in the society in the age group category of below 25 years. 75 percent of the viewers hold the view that there should be inter-caste dining in the society whereas 25 percent of the viewers hold the view that there should not be inter-caste dining in the society in the age group category of 26–35 years. 35.7 percent of the viewers hold the view that there should be inter-caste dining in the society whereas 64.2 percent of the viewers hold the view that there should not be inter-caste dining in the society in the age group category of 36–45 years. 33.3 percent of the viewers hold the view that there should be inter-caste dining in the society whereas 66.6 percent of the viewers hold the view that there should not be inter-caste dining in the society in the age group category of 46 and above years.

It is also evident from the table that 57.5 percent of the total viewers hold the view that there should be inter-caste dining in the society whereas 42.5 percent of the viewers hold the view that there should not be inter-caste dining in the society.

It means that majority of the viewers hold the view that there should be inter-caste dining in the society.

Table – 8.5

Marriages : Inter-Religious Community

Age groups	N	Inter-religious community marriages			
		Yes	%	No	%
Below 25	40	25	62.5	15	37.5
26–35	60	20	33.3	40	66.6
36–45	70	20	28.5	50	71.4
46 and above	30	3	10.0	27	90.0
Total	200	68	34.0	132	66.0

It was asked from the viewers that 'Is Inter-religious community marriages should be encouraged'? The responses obtained from them are presented in table 8.5. It is evident from the table that 62.5 percent of the viewers hold the view that inter-religious community marriages should be encouraged whereas 37.5 percent of the viewers hold the view that inter-religious community marriages should not be encouraged in the age group category of below 25 years. 33.3 percent of the viewers hold the view that inter-religious community marriages should be encouraged whereas 66.6 percent of the viewers hold the view that inter-religious community marriages should not be encouraged in the age group category of 26–35 years. 28.5 percent of the viewers hold the view that inter-religious community marriages should be encouraged whereas 71.4 percent of the viewers hold the view that inter-religious community marriages should not be encouraged in the age group category of 36–45 years. 10 percent of the viewers hold the view that inter-religious community marriages should be encouraged whereas 90 percent of the viewers hold the view that inter-religious community marriages should not be encouraged in the age group category of 46 and above years.

It is also evident from the table that 34 percent of the total viewers hold the view that inter-religious community marriages should be encouraged whereas 66 percent of the total viewers hold the view that inter-religious community marriages should not be encouraged.

It means that majority of the viewers hold the view that inter-religious community marriages should not be encouraged.

Table – 8.6

Friends : Other Religious Community

Age groups	N	Friends from other religious community			
		Yes	%	No	%
Below 25	40	30	75.0	10	25.0

26–35	60	40	66.6	20	33.3
36–45	70	50	71.4	20	28.5
46 and above	30	25	83.3	5	16.6
Total	200	145	72.5	55	27.5

The question was asked to the viewers that 'Have you friends from other religious community'? The responses obtained from them are presented in table 8.6. It is evident from the table that 75 percent of the viewers have friends from other religious community whereas 25 percent of the viewers are without friends from other religious community in the age group category of below 25 years. 66.6 percent of the viewers have friends from other religious community whereas 33.3 percent of the viewers have not any friend from other religious community in the age group category 26–35 years. 71.4 percent of the viewers have their friends from other religious community whereas 28.5 percent of the viewers have not their friends from other religious community in the age group category of 36–45 years. 83.3 percent of the viewers have their friends from other religious community whereas 16.6 percent of the viewers have not their friends from other religious community in the age group category of 46 and above years.

It is also evident from the table that 72.5 percent of the total viewers have their friends from other religious community whereas 27.5 percent of the total viewers do not have their friends from other religious community.

It means that majority of the viewers have their friends from other religious community.

Table – 8.7

Diagnosis by Doctor

Age group	N	Diagnosis by Doctor			
		Yes	%	No	%
Below 25	40	35	87.5	5	12.5
26–35	60	45	75.0	15	25.0
36–45	70	45	64.2	25	35.7
46 and above	30	20	66.6	10	33.3
Total	200	145	72.5	55	27.5

The question was asked to the viewers that 'In case of illness, Do you prefer the Doctor for diagnosis'? The responses obtained from them are presented in table 8.7. It is evident from the table that 87.5 percent of the viewers do prefer the doctor for diagnosis whereas 12.5 percent of the viewers do not prefer the Doctor for diagnosis in case of illness in the age group category of below 25 years. 75 percent of the viewers do prefer the Doctor for diagnosis in case of illness whereas 25 percent of the viewers do not prefer the Doctor for the diagnosis in case of illness in the age group category of 26–35 years. 64.2 percent of the viewers do prefer the Doctor for the diagnosis in case of illness whereas 35.7 percent of the viewers do not prefer the doctor for the diagnosis in case of illness in the age group category of 36–45 years. 66.6 percent of the viewers do prefer the Doctor for the diagnosis in case of illness whereas 33.3 percent of the viewers do not prefer the Doctor for the diagnosis in case of illness in the age group category of 46 and above years.

It is also evident from the table that 72.5 percent of the total viewers do prefer the Doctor for the diagnosis in case of illness whereas 27.5 percent of the total viewers do not prefer the doctor for the diagnosis in case of illness.

It means that majority of the viewers do prefer the Doctor for the diagnosis in case of illness. It is important to note here that 27.5 percent of the viewers do prefer 'the Ojha etc.' in case of their illness.

Table – 8.8

Condition of individual depends on fate

Age groups	N	Depends on fate			
		Yes	%	No	%
Below 25	40	15	37.5	25	62.5
26–35	60	20	33.3	40	66.6
36–45	70	40	57.1	30	42.8
46 and above	30	25	83.3	5	16.6
Total	200	100	50.0	100	50.0

The question asked to the viewers was that 'Are the conditions of individual depends on fate'? The responses obtained from them are presented in table 8.8. It is evident from the table that 37.5 percent of the viewers hold the view that the conditions of individual depends on fate whereas 62.5 percent of the viewers hold the view that the conditions of individual do not depends on fate in the age group category of below 25 years. 33.3 percent of the viewers hold the view that the conditions of individual depends on fate whereas 66.6 percent of the viewers hold the view that the conditions of individual do not depends on fate in the age group category of 26–35 years. 57.1 percent of the viewers hold the view that the conditions of individual depends on fate whereas 42.8 percent of the viewers hold the view that the conditions of individual do not depends on fate in the age group category of 36–45 years. 83.3 percent of the viewers hold the view that the conditions of individual depends on fate whereas 16.6 percent of the viewers hold the view that the conditions of individual do not depends on fate in the age group category of 46 and above years.

It is also evident from the table that 50 percent of the total viewers hold the view that the conditions of individual depends on fate whereas 50 percent of the viewers hold the view that the conditions of individual do not depends on fate.

It is important to note that 50 percent of the viewers hold the view that the conditions of individual depends on hard labour.

Table – 8.9

Controlled by God

Age groups	N	Actions : Controlled by God			
		Yes	%	No	%
Below 25	40	40	100.0	–	–
26–35	60	60	100.0	–	–
36–45	70	70	100.0	–	–
46 and above	30	30	100.0	–	–
Total	200	200	100.0	–	–

The next question asked to the viewers was that 'Are all actions controlled by God'? The responses obtained from them are presented in table 8.9. It is evident from the table that 100 percent of the viewers in each category of age group hold the view that all actions are controlled by God.

Table – 8.10

Doordarshan : Continuity and Change

Age groups	N	Impact of Doordarshan on Continuity and Change			
		Yes	%	No	%
Below 25	40	40	100.0	–	–
26–35	60	60	100.0	–	–
36–45	70	70	100.0	–	–
46 and above	30	30	100.0	–	–
Total	200	200	100.0	–	–

The question asked to the viewers was that 'Is there any impact of Doordarshan on continuity and change'? The responses obtained from them are presented in table 8.10. It is evident from the table that 100 percent of the viewers in each category of age group hold the view that there is impact of Doordarshan on continuity and change.

7

Conclusion

Exposure to the mass media is an important variable in large-scale directed social change, and modernization in developing societies, the mass media makes indispensable impetus to psycho-political life of a transitional society via 'the minds and hearts of its people'. It teaches people by depicting few and strange situations and familiarizes them with a range of opinions among which they can choose. A typical statement about the modernizing effects of media exposure is powder makers: 'the mass media introduced to Africans another form of reality - a world and peoples beyond their experiences. Similarly, Lerner states that 'Increasingly, in the villages and hamlets of the world, the mass media are bringing 'Strange new worlds' into the traditional environment of rural people. In transitional societies, the learning of modern political roles (political socialization) comes in part from later experience with the mass media system, since media is a major purveyor of modern influences. Lerner notes that public communication activates new modes of socialization. A new political class is recruited that aggregates new interests.

The nature and scope of the mass media differs from one country to another. In the communication process in transitional societies, the urban–village levels are not closely integrated. In less developed countries, it reaches only to smaller audiences, such as university student, members of professions, the middle class, and urban dwellers. This is due to the availability, and the degree of Government control. Communication can be direct or indirect, face to face contact versus the impersonal channels. Recent years have shown a tremendous growth in mass media techniques. By using these new techniques such as radio and television, the Governments of developing countries are reaching larger audiences. Rogers and Svenning has rightly said that 'larger mass media audiences, accompanied by high levels of mass media exposure per capita, can be expected to lead those exposed to more favorable attitudes toward change and development, to greater awareness of political events and to more knowledge of technical information.

It has been found that mass media is correlated to other variables of modernization such as literacy, political knowledge, empathy, innovativeness, aspirations, and achievement motive.

The approach and strategy of tribal development for the development of tribals living in areas of their concentration are different from that of the development of dispersed tribal population.

Infrastructual development plays a significant role for the development of tribals living in areas of their concentration. Therefore, area development with focus on the development of tribal communities was evolved in relation to the development in tribal areas. Area planning approach has been adopted as the sub-plan areas identified contain non-tribal population in addition to the tribal population. But the focus is on tribals. A tribal community, in its home territory, initially has full command over the local resources. In the predominantly tribal areas, this situation has not been disturbed to a large extent at least in practice, if not in law. On the other hand, command over resources in the case of dispersed tribal is now extremely limited. Therefore, there is a qualitative change in the initial conditions for tribal development in the situation compared to the predominantly tribal areas. It is easier to prevent deprivation and 'running down' of a system than to restore the original state once it has been disturbed.

The case of dispersed tribals therefore is placed on a different footing. Infrastructural development in areas with dispersed tribal population cannot be treated as a part of the tribal development programme. It should form an integral part of the general development programme of the area... The loss of command over resources and dispersal of population itself, sometimes result in social regression. Thus in the case of dispersed tribals, development has to be planned taking the group or the family as a unit.

Lot of things has been said and written about tribals and their place in the Indian society, their emotional integration,, their problems, welfare, etc. It is often said that the tribals are a section of the greater Indian society and it is not possible to build a strong prosperous Indian nation without them, by keeping this particular section weak and undeveloped. Because the weaker and less advanced section would retard the overall progress of the country.

Nobody can deny the fact that a good many socio–religious customs, still existing among the Indian communities, were borrowed from the tribal society in the long past. But very few of the present day Indians are quite conversant with them. We kept the tribals aloof for centuries, did not try to initiate an area for developing social co-operation and even did not care to give them a position in our social set up. The British rule too has been responsible for keeping the tribals aloof.

After independence, certain constitutional provisions and safeguards have been provided and developmental activities have been undertaken for their welfare so that may become a strong integrated section of the Indian society within a specific period of time.

The gradual process of identification with the greater Indian nation got set back while the identification on the ethnic level started becoming popular. It seems that the overall outcome of the situation is due to the non appreciation of the tribal problems, lack of proper sympathy for them and also due to viewing the welfare work as a relief measure. This sort of wrong approach is mainly responsible for the frustration in this sphere. We need a group of sincere, devoted workers, with imagination, integrity and perseverance, who can give leadership for achieving a well balanced social cooperation.

There is no doubt that by spending crores of rupees, energy and time the country is successful in bringing certain outward changes, in educational, economic, social as well as material levels but how far a change has taken place in their psychological level is a matter of guessing. Not to speak of the psychology of the tribals, what is our psychological relations towards tribals? Has it changed? on the basis of this study, I can say that Doordarshan has done lot of work in this direction to answer these questions.

The spread of modern education with the wider scope of employment opportunity among the tribal population would accelerate integration process. The educated tribals would also help in accelerating the process of integration by giving their able leadership to their community people.

II

The present work is related to impact of 'Doordarshan' on tribals. The prime objectives of this work is to analyse the relationship between tribal community and Doordarshan and their exposure to this media, to analyse the impact of Doordarshan on tribals towards educational, cultural, economic as well as political developments and to analyse the impact of Doordarshan on tribals towards continuïty and change.

The present work is divided into seven chapters. The first chapter 'Introduction' is related to presentation of the subject, concept, tribe, tribalism, de-tribalization, earlier literature, main objectives and the microscopic study. The second chapter is 'Doordarshan : A profile' is related with the profile of Doordarshan. The third chapter 'Doordarshan : A microscopic study' is related with the methods which is used in this study. The hypothesis of the study, interview schedule, sampling, observation and the research design–descriptive research design has been analysed in this chapter. The data related to the viewers has been analysed in the fourth chapter 'Doordarshan : An overview of the viewers'. The information related to Doordarshan and other mass media as well as their exposure to these media has been analysed in the fifth chapter 'Doordarshan and Other Mass Media'. The educational development, social development, economic and occupational development, cultural development, political development and continuity and change among the tribal community with relation to the impact of Doordarshan has been analysed in the sixth chapter

'Doordarshan : Change and Development'. The seventh chapter is the 'Conclusion' of this work. It has been presented with the help of tables and its analysis for the systematic study in fourth, fifth and chapter sixth.

In the present work, 200 viewers participated and gave their views on Doordarshan. The information were also collected on the basis of secondary sources, like papers, magazines etc.

III

On the basis of these facts, the conclusion of this work is as follows :

Doordarshan : An overview of the viewers

In the present work, the viewers belong to different age ranges from below 25 years to 46 and above years. 35 percent of the viewers are from the age group of 36 to 45 years, 30 percent of the viewers are from the age group of 26 to 35 years, 20 percent of the viewers are from the age group of below 25 years and 15 percent of the viewers are from the age group of 46 and above years. It means the majority of viewers are from the young age group.

In this study, there are 50 percent of the male viewers and 50 percent of the female viewers. It means that men and women are equally selected by the investigator.

A majority of 80 percent of the viewers are from rural background whereas 20 percent of the viewers are from the urban background. It is classified on the basis of birth-place. It means that the viewers from rural background use to come town for their work. It shows the mobility among the tribal people of this area.

A majority of 40 percent of the viewers are educated up to secondary level. Only 2.5 percent of the viewers are educated up to above post-graduation level, 5 percent of the viewers are educated up to post-graduation level, 20 percent of the viewers are educated up to matriculation level, 17.5 percent of the viewers are educated up to graduation level whereas 15 percent of the viewers are illiterate. It means that the level of education is still not satisfactory among the tribal people.

55 percent of the total viewers belong to Sarana religion whereas 45 percent of the viewers belong to Christianity.

A majority of 62.5 percent of the viewers are married, 35 percent of the viewers are unmarried. Only 2.5 percent of the viewers are widow or divorced.

30 percent of the viewers are in service, 25 percent of the viewers are working as labourers, 25 percent of the viewers studying or doing work for house-hold affairs, 10 percent of the viewers are engaged in agriculture and remaining 10 percent of the viewers are doing self-business. It means that the viewers were included from different occupations in the present study.

In the present work, 30 percent of the viewers are earning below rupees 2000/- per month, 25 percent of the viewers are earning rupees 2001 to 4000/- per month, 20 percent of the viewers are earning rupees 4001 to 6000/- per month, 12.5 percent of the viewers are earning rupees 6001 to 8000/- per month, 7.5 percent of the viewers are earning rupees 8001 to 10000/- per month and only 5 percent of the viewers are earning rupees above 10000/- per month. This income consists both the personal and family income per month. It means that the economic condition is not satisfactory among tribal people, universe under this study.

A majority of 65 percent of the viewers are living in nuclear family whereas 35 percent of the viewers are living in joint family. It means that the family structure is changing very fast among the tribal people of this area.

15 percent of the viewers are living with below 4 members in their families, 30 percent of the viewers are living with 5 to 7 members, 35 percent of the viewers are living with 8 to 10 members, 15 percent of the viewers are living with 11 to 13 members and only 5 percent of the viewers are living with 13 members in their families.

A majority of 55 percent of the viewers have own building whereas 45 percent of the viewers live in rented buildings.

The viewers were included from the different tribal groups in the present study. 30 percent of the viewers are Oraons, 30 percent of the viewers are Mundas, 20 percent of the viewers are Santhals, 10 percent of the viewers are Hos, 5 percent of the viewers are Kharias and 5 percent of the viewers are from the other than these tribal groups.

Doordarshan and Other Mass Media

In the present study, many questions were asked about their exposure towards the mass media. It is important that 100 percent of the viewers are viewing television. It is also interesting that 21 percent of the viewers are viewing television regularly, 24.5 percent of the viewers are viewing a number of times a week, 26 percent of the viewers are viewing at least once a week and 28.5 percent of the viewers are viewing television occasionally.

It is important that 100 percent of the viewers are viewing Doordarshan whereas only 45.5 percent of the viewers are viewing other satellite/cable channels. It is also important that 17 percent of the viewers are viewing mainly current affairs, 30 percent of the viewers are viewing mainly Films/Dance/Cultural programmes, 17 percent of the viewers are viewing mainly programmes related to agriculture and rural developments and 11.5 percent of the viewers are viewing mainly other than these programmes of Doordarshan.

A majority of 70 percent of the viewers hold the view that Doordarshan produces good effects, 23 percent of the viewers hold the view that it produces both good and bad effects and only 7 percent of the viewers hold the view that it produces bad effects. A majority of the viewers hold the view that Doordarshan not only provides much needed entertainment to the rural and urban people but also exposes them to social, economic. Religious and cultural themes and consciousness. The documentaries fulfill a much desired need for information. The viewers still remember 'Ramayana', 'Mahabharat', 'Rajani', Hamlog', 'Buniyad' etc.

In relation to other satellite/cable channels, 13.5 percent of the viewers hold the view that it produces good effects, 66.5 percent of the viewers hold the view that it produces bad effects and 20 percent of the viewers hold the view that it produces both good and bad effects. It means that in comparison to Doordarshan, it is not accepted by the majority of the tribal people.

A majority of 52 percent of the tribal people are viewing cinema. Among them, 8.6 percent of the viewers are viewing once a week, 25 percent of the viewers are viewing once a month and 66.3 percent of the viewers are viewing occasionally. 20 percent of the viewers hold the view that cinema produces good effects, 29 percent of the viewers hold the view that it produces both good and bad effects and a majority of 51 percent of the viewers hold the view that cinema produces bad effects.

As far as the exposure to the newspaper is concerned, 49 percent of the viewers are reading newspapers. Remaining of the viewers are not interested in newspapers. 38 percent of the viewers hold the view that newspaper produces good effects, 9.5 percent of the viewers hold the view that it produces bad effects and majority of 52.5 percent of the viewers hold the view that it produces both good and bad effects.

Exposure to the radio listening, 95 percent of the viewers are listening radio programmes. 70 percent of the viewers hold the view that radio produces good effects, 26 percent of the viewers hold the view that it produces both good and bad effects and only 4 percent of the viewers hold the view that radio produces bad effects.

As exposure to the magazine reading is concerned, only 24 percent of the viewers are reading magazines. 28.5 percent of the viewers hold the view that magazines produces good effects, 15.5 percent of the viewers hold the view that it produces bad effects and a majority of 56 percent of the viewers hold the view that it produces both good and bad effects.

The viewers are not very much exposed to the computer/internet media. Only 9.5 percent of the viewers are knowing computer/internet operating.

It means that the tribal people, who are living or working in Ranchi town are very much exposed to the Doordarshan in comparison to other mass media. The programmes of Doordarshan are very much popular among these tribal people. It is playing vital role in the life of tribal people in this area. Now it is becoming one of the main agencies in the development process in the society.

Doordarshan : Change and Development

As far as educational development is concerned, 51.1 percent of the viewers are educated from those institutions which are managed or controlled by the government whereas 48.8 percent of the viewers are educated from those institutions which are managed or controlled by the non-government agencies or by the different missions. It means that non-government agencies or different missions are also working to educate these tribal people.

There was co-education in the case of 76.4 percent of the viewers. 87.5 percent of the viewers hold the view that there should be co-education in the educational institutions. It means that tribal people are progressive in this direction.

58.8 percent of the viewers are satisfied with their syllabus of the education. It means that the tribal people are liking the changing syllabus according to the changing situations.

31.5 percent of the viewers hold the view that the culture of the campus is good. It means that still culture of the campus is good.

75 percent of the viewers are interested in sports and its activities and 67.5 percent of the viewers are interested in extra curricular activities. I means that the study is necessary with the sports activities.

It is interesting that 94 percent of the viewers are interested to educate their children. 32.4 percent of the viewers hold the view that the medium of education of their children should be mother tongue, 61.7 percent of the viewers hold the view that the medium of education should be English and only 5.8 percent of the viewers hold the view that the medium of education of their children should be Hindi. It means that tribal people are progressive and very much anxious to come into main stream.

It is interesting that 100 percent of the viewers hold the view that there are a lot of impact of Doordarshan on education and educational activities. It is but natural that Doordarshan produces a lot of educational programmes and programmes related to educational activities. So, these tribal people are very much influenced by these programmes.

As far as social consciousness of these tribal people are concerned, 75 percent of the viewers hold the view that women should have equal right as men. 76.5 percent of the viewers hold the view that family planning programme is right. 67.5 percent of the viewers hold the view that women's liberation is right. It means that these tribal people are very much conscious about the status and right of women in the society. The status of women is very high in the tribal society.

In this study, 69 percent of the viewers hold the view that inter–caste marriages should be encouraged. It is interesting that there are so many viewers hold the view that inter–tribal marriages should also be encouraged. 85 percent of the viewers hold the view that marriage system is changing. It means that the views of these tribal people are very progressive and they are in the process of modernization.

In the present work, 94.5 percent of the viewers hold the view that the family structure is changing. It means that there is the process of industrialization, urbanization, occupational mobility and the process of modernization.

It is also interesting that 100 percent of the viewers hold the view that there are impact of Doordarshan on social consciousness and development of an individual or the society. It means that these tribal people are very much influenced by the programmes of Doordarshan.

In relation to the economic and occupational development, 64.6 percent of the viewers are satisfied with their occupation/job. 58.4 percent of the viewers hold the view that they like to change their occupation/ job in near future. 52.5 percent of the viewers like to go to other places for better working conditions. It means that there is occupational mobility among these tribal people. The working conditions are not very good.

32.5 percent of the viewers are satisfied with their standard of living but majority of the viewers are not satisfied with their standard of living. It means that these tribal people are living in very low conditions.

In the present work, 69 percent of the viewers are aware about the economic programmes of government. It means that due to awareness, these tribal people are knowing the various economic and welfare programmes of the government. It is also because Doordarshan produces a lot of awareness programmes.

In the present work, 94 percent of the viewers are participating in various festivals. It means that these tribal people are still tradition oriented. Festivals are the main part of their life.

In the present work, 75 percent of the viewers are liking to changes in dress pattern. 94 percent of the viewers are interested in music and musical instruments. It is interesting that 100 percent of the viewers are liking the changes in their food habits. It shows that the dress pattern and food habits are changing very fast in the society. Music and musical instruments are the life of these tribal people. Keeping in view, Doordarshan produces various programmes related to the music and dance.

52.5 percent of the viewers are the members of the clubs or other cultural organizations. It means that these tribal people are also participating in the activities of clubs or other cultural organizations. It shows the progressive attitude of these tribal people of this area.

In the present work, 42.5 percent of the viewers believe in magic etc. It means that these tribal people to some extent, do believe in these activities. It shows that still they are tradition oriented.

It is also interesting that 100 percent of the viewers hold the view that there are impact of Doordarshan on their culture and cultural activities because Doordarshan produces various programmes related to local culture and cultural activities. In this way, these tribal people are very much influenced by the programmes of Doordarshan.

In relation to political development. 32.5 percent of the viewers are related to political parties. It means that there is political participation. It shows that these tribal people are in the process of modernization to some extent.

In this work, 50 percent of the viewers did cast their vote in the last election. 46 percent of the viewers hold the view that women did participate in the last election. It also means that there is political participation. In shows that these tribal people are becoming progressive and they are politically conscious.

In the present work, 100 percent of the viewers hold the view that reservation is necessary and also hold the view that there are impact of Doordarshan on political activities and concerned development. It means that these tribal people are very much conscious on the reservation issue. It shows that these tribal people are highly conscious about their right. It also shows that these tribal people are very much influenced by the various programmes of Doordarshan.

In relation to the continuity and change, 100 percent of the viewers believe in religion. It means that these tribal people are still belief oriented, traditional and orthodoxy in this sense.

In the present work, 75 percent of the viewers hold the view that old values are changing. 45 percent of the viewers hold the view that we should honour the traditional ways. It means that the tribal society is in transition. Values are changing very fast. These tribal people are still tradition oriented but they are in the process of modernization.

57.5 percent of the viewers hold the view that there should be inter-caste dining in the society. 34 percent of the viewers hold the view that inter-religious community marriages should be encouraged. 72.5 percent of the viewers have their friends from other religious community. It means that these tribal people are in the process of modernization. It shows the rational outlook of these tribal people.

In the present work, 72.5 percent of the viewers do prefer the Doctor for the diagnosis in case of their illness. It means that these tribal people are in the process of modernization. It shows the rational outlook of these tribal people to some extent.

In this work, 50 percent of the viewers hold the view that the conditions of an individual depends on fate. 100 percent of the viewers hold the view that all actions are controlled by the God. It means that these tribal people are still tradition oriented. It shows that tradition is deep rooted in the tribal society.

In the light of above factual conclusion, The tribal people under study are in the process of modernization. The tradition-modernity continuum exists. These tribal people are rational in their outlook and approach but slightly lagging behind in their practice. Now the programmes of the state government has accelerated the developmental process very fast. These tribal people are very much influenced by the various programmes of Doordarshan and Doordarshan produces very good impact on the tribal society of the area. Now it has become a part of the tribal life.

Bibliography

Amberoo, U., 'Higher ·Education and Occupational Mobility among the Scheduled Castes', Journal of Higher Education, 1(3), 1976.

Adhikari, A.K., 'Society and World View of the Birhor', Calcutta, 1984.

Agnew, Vijay., 'Elite Women in Indian Politics' Vikas Publishing House, New Delhi, 1979.

Altekar, A.S., 'The Position of Women in Hindu Civilization', Motilal Banarsidas Publishers, Varanasi, 1956.

Bhardwaj, G., 'Socio-Political Movements Among the Tribes of India', in S.C.Dube (ed.) Tribal Heritage of India, Vol.1, Vikas Publishing House, New Delhi, 1977.

Bhandra, R.K., 'Revitalization Movement among the Gonds of Madhya Pradesh', Eastern Anthropologist, 30 (2), 1977.

Basu, S.K. and Sahu, R.N., 'The Mundas–A Profile' Calcutta, 1987.

Bhowmick, P.K., 'The Lodhas of West Bengal' Calcutta, 1963.

——— 'Dynamics of Tribal Development', New Delhi, 1991.

——— 'Education for Tribal Women : A Suggestion', in Tribal Women and Development (ed.) by Singh and others, Udaipur, 1985.

Bose, N.K., 'Some Indian Tribes', National Book Trust, New Delhi, 1972.

——— 'Tribal Life in India', National Book Trust, New Delhi, 1971.

Bose, Pradeep Kumar, 'Stratification among Tribals in Gujrat', Economic and Political Weekly, February 7, 1981.

Banerjee, Mangobinda, 'An Historical Outline of Pre-British Chotanagpur (From Earliest Times to 1765)', Educational Publications, Ranchi, 1993 (Reprinted).

Chitnis, S., 'Reservation in Education : The Policy and the Practice', Pear for the Seminar on Removal of Untouchability, Ahmedabad, 1979.

——— 'Education as the Instrument for Social Reconstruction : The Case of Untouchables in India', Paper presented for VIII World Congress of Sociology, Toronto, 1974.

Chauhan, I.S., 'Culture Change in Tribal Life', Economic and Political Weekly (special number), 7 (31-3) : 1675-81, 1970.

Chu, Goodwin C., 'When Television Comes to a Traditional Village', Paper presented at the Pacific Chapter of the American Association for Public Opinion Research, San Francisco, 1966.

Clor, Harry M., 'The Mass Media and Modern Democracy', Chicago : Rand Mc-Nalley College Publishing Company, 1974.

Dube, S.C. 'Tribal Heritage of India', Vol.1, Ethnicity, Identity and Interaction, Vikas Publishing House, New Delhi, 1977.

Dhan, R.O., 'Tribal Movements in Chotanagpur', in S.C.Mullic (ed.), Dissant, Protest and Reform in Indian Civilization, Indian Institute of Advanced Study, Simla, 1977.

Desai, I.P., 'The Tribal Autonomy Movement in South Gujrat', K.S. Singh (ed.) Tribal Movements, Manohar, Vol. II, New Delhi, 1983.

Das, Biswajit., 'Mass Media', Report on Fifty Years of Communication Growth in India, Mimeohraphed, 1997.

Dissanayake, W., 'Communication, Knowledge and a Post-Industrial Society : The Need for Values - Centred Approach', in Christian Academy (ed.), World Community in Post-Industrial Society, Seoul : Wooseok Publishing Co., 1988.

Deuschmann, Paul J., 'The Mass Media in an Underdeveloped Village', Journalism Quarterly, 40, 1963.

Elwin, V., 'Tribal Women' in Indian Women (ed.) by D. Jain, New Delhi, 1975.

——— 'Religion of a Tribe', Oxford University Press, London, 1955.

Frey, Frederick W., 'The Mass Media and Rural Development in Turkey', Cambridge : MIT, Centre for International Studies Research Report 3, 1966.

Ghurye, G.S., 'The Scheduled Tribes', Popular Book Depot., Bombay, 1969.

Gore, M.S., 'Urbanization and Family Change', Popular Prakashan, Bombay, 1968.

Gupta, Dipankar., 'Mistaken Modernity' Harper Collins Publishers Pvt Ltd., New Delhi, 2000.

Jha, K.N., 'Women Towards Modernization', Janki Prakashan, Patna, 1985.

Jha, B.N., 'Adhunik Bharat Mein Jati Avam Shiksha', Janki Prakashan, Patna, 1985.

Kroeber, A.L., 'The Nature of Culture', Chicago University Press, 1952.

Lerner, Daniel., 'The Passing of Traditional Society : Modernizing the Middle East', The Free Press, New York, 1966.

Mishra, P.K., 'Patterns of Inter-Tribal Relation', in S.C.Dube (ed.) Tribal Heritage of India, Vol.I, Vikas Publishing House, New Delhi, 1977.

Mahapatra, L.K., 'Social Movements among Tribes of Eastern India', Sociology 18 (1), 1968.

Merton, R.K., 'Social Theory and Social Structure, Illinois, The Free Press, 1957.

Madhok, Sujata., 'Women, Media and Empowerment', in Empowering The Indian Women, Promilla Kapur, Publication Division, Government of India, 2001.

Orans, Martin., 'The Santal : A Tribe in Search of a Great Tradition', Detroit, Wayne University Press, 1965.

Prakash, Amit., 'Jharkhand', Politics of Development and Identity, Orient Longman Limited, Hyderabad, 2001.

Prasad, S.S., 'Tribal Women Labourers : Aspects of Economic and Physical Exploitation', Gian Publishing House, Delhi, 1988.

Roy, S.C., 'The Birhors', Ranchi, 1925.

——— 'The Kharias', Vol.I & II, Ranchi, 1937.

——— 'Oraon Religion and Customs', Ranchi, 1928.

——— 'Oraons of Chotanagpur', Calcutta, 1915.

——— 'The Mundas and their Country', Asia Publishing House, Bombay, 1968.

Roy, A.K., 'Jharkhand aur Lalkhand', Dhanbad, 1981.

Sachchidananda, 'Tribal Women in the Throes of Development', in Tribal Women and Development (ed.) by Singh and others, Udaipur, 1985.

——— 'Culture Change in Tribal Bihar', Bookland, Calcutta, 1964.

Srinivas, M.N., 'Social Change in Modern India', Berkeley California University Press, U.S.A., 1966.

——— 'The Changing Position of India's Women', Oxford University Press, New Delhi, 1978.

Sinha, Surajit, 'Transformation of Tribal Society in Modern India', Devraj Chanana Memorial Lecturer, 1973. (on published)

——— 'Tribe-Caste and Tribe–Peasant Continue in Central India', Man in Asia, Vol.45, March, 1965.

Sinha, Arun, 'Bihar Resurgent Adivasi', Economic and Political Weekly, 9 Sept., 1978.

Singh, Yogendra, 'Modernization of Indian Tradition', Thomson Press, New Delhi, 1973.

——— 'Social Stratification and Change in India', Manohar, New Delhi, 1977.

——— 'Indian Sociology', Vistaar Publications, New Delhi, 1986.

——— 'Culture Change in India', Rawat Publications, Jaipur and New Delhi, 2000.

Singh, K.S., 'Tribal Situation in India', (ed.) The Indian Institute of Advanced Study (IIAS) Simla, 1972.

——— 'Tribal Movements in India' Vol.I (ed.) Manohar, New Delhi, 1982.

——— 'Tribal Movements in India', Vol.II (ed.), Manohar, New Delhi, 1983.

——— 'Tribal Society in India' Manohar, New Delhi, 1985.

Sharma, K.L., 'Reconceptualising Caste, Class and Tribe', Rawat Publications, Jaipur and New Delhi, 2001.

Sahay, K.N., 'Change of Tribal Identity in Chotanagpur', Kishor Vidya Niketan, Varanasi, 1985.

Saran, A.B., 'Tribal Studies', Ranchi Offset Printers, Ranchi, 1978.

Schiller, H.I., 'Current Views of Information and Media Power', in Christian Academy (ed.), The World Community in Post–Industrial Society, Seoul : Wooseok Publishing Co., 1988.

Tylor, E.B., 'Primitive Culture', J. Murry, London, 1971.

Vidyarthi, L.P., 'Impact of Industrialization in India : A Case Study of Tribal Bihar', R.P.C., Planning Commission, Government of India, New Delhi, 1970.

----- 'Dynamics of Tribal Leadership in Bihar', Research Project on Changing Leadership in a Tribal Society', 1967-71, Kitab Mahal, Allahabad, 1978.

——— 'Cultural Contour of Tribal Bihar', 1964.

Whiting, Gordon C., 'Empathy, Mass Media and Modernization : A Study of Rural Brazil', Ph.D. Thesis, Michigan State University, 1967.

Periodicals

The Adivasi', Tribal Research Institute, Bhubneshwar.

'The Adivasi', Public Relation Department, Government of Bihar, Ranchi.

'Economic and Political Weekly', Bombay.

'Adivasi Gujrat', Tribal Training and Research Institute, Gujrat Vidyapeeth, Ahmadabad.

'Man in India', Ranchi.

'Society Today', Darbhanga.

'Bulletin of Jharkhand Tribal Welfare Research Institute', Ranchi.

'Sociological Bulletin', New Delhi (Journal of India Sociological Society).

'Doordarshan India 2000' (Prasar Bharti, Broadcasting Corporation of India, Audience Research Unit, New Delhi).

'Doordarshan in Jharkhand' (Facts at a Glance '2000), Audience Research Unit, Doordarshan Kendra, Ranchi.

Newspapers

The Times of India, New Delhi

The Indian Express, New Delhi

The Hindustan Times, New Delhi

Ranchi Express, Ranchi

Prabhat Khabar, Ranchi

Hindustan, Ranchi

INDEX

Index

N

O

P

R

S

T

❑ ❑ ❑